James Webb Rogers

Parthenon

1st Part

James Webb Rogers

Parthenon
1st Part

ISBN/EAN: 9783742875600

Manufactured in Europe, USA, Canada, Australia, Japa

Cover: Foto ©Lupo / pixelio.de

Manufactured and distributed by brebook publishing software (www.brebook.com)

James Webb Rogers

Parthenon

PUBLISHER'S NOTICE.

The author of "Parthenon" has been lately represented in the Pan-Electric controversy, as an ignorant and vulgar person, but the following extracts, which we take from his New York publisher's notice appended to the second edition of his "Greek Slave," will indicate that his political enemies have, perhaps, underrated him :

"The most Rev. Archbishop introduced him to the audience * * very eloquent."—*Catholic Telegraph.*

"Introduced by Rev. Wm. Quinn, of St. Peter's Church, to a large and appreciative audience. Was frequently interrupted by loud applause. Able and erudite."—*N. Y. Herald.*

"Great ability as a lecturer—eloquent—interesting—popular."—*Rev. I. T. Hecker, Editor " Catholic World."*

"Great success." "Unusually delighted audience." "Eloquent and live man."—*N. Y. Freeman's Journal,*

"Maintained a learned and subtle argument."—*N. Y. Times.*

"Rising to the loftiest flights of eloquence."—*New Orleans Times.*

"Humorous, pathetic and impassioned; evidently born to move men."—*New Orleans Picayune.*

"Introduced by Rev. Thos. Foley, V. G., the most Rev. Archbishop Spaulding, the Bishop of North Carolina, and about twenty of the Rev. clergy on the stage. * * Frank and highly intellectual."—*Baltimore Mirror.*

"Graceful manner; rich imagery; eloquent delivery; highly ornate and classic."—*St. Louis Times.*

"Nous avons rarement rencontré dans un même homme autant des qualites qui font le véritable orateur. Voix flexible et sonore, gestes admirable de naturel, style plein d'images et de nerf, et un cœur contenu d'ou falait le sentiment avec une force qui souléve l'auditoire et l'entraine absolument.—*Nouveau Monde, Montreal.*

"Finished speaker. * * * Manner, gestures, antecedents and honesty all conspired to interest and edify."—*Cincinnati Telegraph.*

"An immense audience assembled at Greenlaw Opera House to hear him. * * * Spell-bound for two hours."—*Memphis Appeal.*

"Edifice packed * * * may he receive as hearty a welcome wherever he may go as has been given him in New York."—*N. Y. Tablet.*

"A fine intellectual and oratorical effort."—*Newark Register.*

"Introduced by Bishop McQuade. Spoke extemporaneously, with great force and eloquence."—*Rochester Union and Advertiser.*

"Handled his subject logically and powerfully * * * with a conciseness and clearness rarely heard."—*Wheeling Daily Register.*

"He possesses, in an eminent degree, the peculiar faculty of fixing the attention and interesting the feeling of his hearers. From the commencement to the close, his discourses are a succession of brilliant and sparkling thoughts, with occasional outbursts of impassionate declamation."

"A beautiful poem, indicating the author's learning and refinement." —*N. Y. Tablet.*

"The Southern press has been for several weeks filled with laudatory notices of this poem."—*Mobile Advertiser and Register.*

"A casket of rare gems, in the guise of a poem, presented to the public, which we have just finished reading. Our limits will not permit a merited review of this lengthy and brilliant production, but we would say to those whose souls are attuned to the warblings of genuine poesy, to read and admire it for themselves. It is a story of intense passion, and from beginning to end is luminous with genius. In this thrilling narrative is blended, with a master's hand, the travels of the author in the Mediterranean sea, and his impressions of Italy, Sardinia, Carthage, &c. The apostrophe to Italy is very nearly inimitable in its sublimity and pathos. 'Blue domed and beautiful,' the poet's eye sees her glory as we do the pomp of riven sunset clouds, after the storm has spent its fury. We are literally baptized in a sea of ineffable grandeur as we are floated back to the shrines of 'the world's dead mistress,' and when our ardor cools, still, as the author expresses it,

'Her thousand colors on our spirits lie,
Soft as the stars in yonder tranquil sky.'"
—*Selma Times.*

"Spoken highly of by the American press.—*London Tablet.*

We find, in another publication, that the author was lately commended to President Cleveland for the office of assistant attorney in the Department of Justice, by "His Grace, the Archbishop of Baltimore, Primate of the United States, and now His Eminence Cardinal Gibbons; His Grace, the Archbishop of Philadelphia, and their Lordships, the Bishop of Albany and Buffalo, together with many other dignitaries, both in Church and State; the greatest of living Generals; Senators; Congressmen; presidents and professors of colleges; the most eminent of lawyers, among them Hon. Arthur McArthur, of the Supreme Court of the District of Columbia, and the leading members of the Washington bar, where the author has practised law for the last ten years."

PREFACE TO "PARTHENON."

This Poem, in four parts, describes *Parthenon* and the surrounding manors—her own external beauty, and inner life: giving at the same time, a sketch of *the four Seasons*, one in each part.

Whether poetry or not, many of the verses inculcate morality, and may rise above the ordinary sensational sermon.

I leave it in the groves of Parthenon, where many an unseen flower offers incense to the skies!—at any rate being finished at midnight on Xmas eve, it will last as long as the Xmas tree, to cheer the home it describes; Exalting the Blessed Virgin, while it honors the Catholic Church, and defends christianity.

DEDICATION

Without their knowledge, consent or approval, I take the liberty (but with reverence and affection) of dedicating these verses to

THE SOCIETY OF JESUS.

"What!" exclaims poor Ingersoll, "dedicate your poem, seemingly American, to a *foreign* society, and to America's worst enemy?" Not to "a foreign society," but to the daring heroes who once owned, by right of discovery, the greater part of the United States and Canada; who threw open their hospitable doors to your fathers and prohibited persecution, gave peaceful homes to the persecuted Quaker and all the waters of the Chesapeake to the most enthusiastic Baptist. Yes, the Jesuits. Their bleeding steps may still be traced from Chesapeake Bay to the Rocky Mountains, and from the Lake of the Woods to the Gulf of Mexico. Not "America's worst enemy," but her best friend. I behold them flying from nation to nation, like Joseph, Jesus and Mary in their flight to Egypt. They represent "the Holy Family," and should be borne on your shoulders to make the picture complete. The roar of the kingly lion has never deterred them, and they will not now regard his skin, even when it seems to bray! He may browse unrestrained on the greenest grass, but the stars shine on above him forever.

Venerable Fathers, what mighty dynasties have fallen, what crowns and sceptres have mingled with the dust, since your glorious founder, St. Ignatius Loyola, lead the forlorn hope of Christianity, learning and civilization!

His apostles gave to the Oriental world—to China, India, Japan, Thibet and Burmah—a jewel more precious than all their Khoinoors! They checked the madness of Europe in the sixteenth century, trod the burning sands of Africa, and penetrated the wilds of America. Persecuted in one land, they flew to another; but flew only to herald their persecuted master; or died embracing the crucifix with smiles of triumph! Fly on, angelic host!—holier than the angels, in "the new nature" given you. Fly on like eagles, over continents and rivers, lakes, oceans, mountains, to the skies! How do kings still tremble before you, while wicked nations and bad men exclaim: "Let us alone. What have we to do with Thee, Thou Jesus of Nazareth!" for this is the sole thought of unclean souls!

Even while I thus presume to address you, a voice comes from "The Ancient of Days"—from yon "Eternal City:"

"Sint hae litterae Nostrae testes amoris, quo iugitur prosecuti sumus et prosequimur inclytam Societatem Iesu Praedecessoribus Nostris ac Nobis ipsis devotissimam, fecundam, tum sanctimoniae tum sapientiae laude praestantium virorum nutricem, solidae sanaeque altricem doctrinae; quae graves licet propter iustitiam persecutiones perpessa, nunquam in excolenda vinea Domini alacri invictoque animo adlaborare desistit. Pergat igitur bene merita Societas Iesu, ab ipso Concilio Tridentino commendata et a praedecessoribus Nostris praeconio laudum cumulata, pergat in tanta hominum perversitate contra Iesu Christi Ecclesiam suum persequi institutum ad maiorem Dei gloriam sempiternamque animarum salutem; pergat suo ministerio in sacris expeditionibus infideles et haereticos ad veritatis lucem traducere et revocare, inventutem christianis virtutibus bonisque artibus imbuere, philosophicas ac theologicas disciplinas ad mentem Angelici Doctoris tradere. Interea dilectissimam Nobis Societatem Iesu peramanter complectentes, Societatis eiusdem Praeposito Generali et eius Vicario singulisque alumnis Apostolicam impertimus benedictionem.

Datum Romae, apud S. Petrum, sub annulo Piscatoris, die XIII Julii, MDCCCLXXXVI, Pontificatus, Nostri anno nono.

M. CARD. LEDÓCHOWSKI.

Ye watchmen on the ramparts of heaven, behold your work of centuries! Look down on Parthenon, the last of your benefactions! Behold " My Maryland," where your wisdom first proclaimed Religious Liberty ! Pardon her faults and guard her sacred homes! Not Maryland alone, nor St. Mary's cross-teeming valleys, nor Blackstone's Island, still burning with your sacred footprints, could circumscribe your charity. The thunders of Niagara speak to a mighty nation, and remind it of your devotion to the Iriquois! Her smiling rainbows, at the footstool of power, recall the incense ye offered to St. Lawrence, while your mother, the Catholic Church, still spreads sublimer rainbows above the stormy elements of Humanity !

Boston remembers your embassy from Montreal, in the darkest hour of the colonies, when ye came to meet our Jesuit, the mitred Carroll, in the interest of bleeding patriotism, and Catholic soldiers—Kosiusko, La Fayette, Pulaski, Baron de Kalb—leading by land, and Barry on the sea, each hilt twining the rosary about its cross and pointing the brave to victory! What your counsels, your Masses, and your prayers effected eternity may reveal: for your own and kindred orders in the Catholic Church had preserved for Patrick Henry the whole fabric of Common Law, the Equity of the Civil Law, and the sacred volume which taught him to exclaim: " The race is not to the swift, nor the battle to the strong. There is a God who presides over the destinies of nations. I care not, sirs, what other men may choose, but as for me, give me Liberty, or give me Death !"

The Mississippi, discovered by your daring brotherhood—especially La Salle, Marquet and Joliet—still bears to millions the fragrance of your sacrifice, and hundreds of towns and cities and rivers that glitter in the setting sun perpetuate your names.

> " The meanest rill, the mightiest river,
> Rolls mingling with your fame forever!"

Then pardon, illustrious Fathers, in this dedication the presumption of one " unworthy to stoop down and unloose the latchet of your shoes," for your own humility and minor offices invite it. Did you not watch over my father's boyhood in yonder classic temple, then so humble, but now adorning a nation's capital? The same halls have communicated their charity to thousands, who bore it to the multitude, without embracing your creed, which ye guard so sacredly, but obtrude on no one, lest they should trample it under foot. Behold a youthful Corcoran, now sitting at the feet of your Gamaliels in Georgetown, now kindling the torch of his benevolence at your sacred altars, to shine upon the earthquake at Charleston or to pale the fires of Chicago; to light up the world of art for the multitude, blessing the poor with painting, sculpture and poetry; or bearing the author of "Home, Sweet Home" from the ruins of ancient Carthage, to lay him on a mother's bosom in America! Did not the same classic halls inspire my sons with your devotion to letters and your love of truth? Ye have blessed my home at Parthenon by your presence, and touched its jewels with your sanctity—

> Each jewel there a character defined,
> Automic as the sun.
> Yet sparkling as the dews of heaven,
> And melting into one—
> With such a gem I ask for nothing more—
> My heaven and earth in one bright Khoinoor!
> With you to bless us, and a conscience clear;
> I sing the changing seasons of the year!

Epitome of Parthenon.

Spring.

Sweet Spring sat listening to her feathered throng,
While gazed upon her face, the violet blue;
The redbird trembled with voluptuous song
To the young flowers—for he had learned to woo,
And taught me, Leila, how to sing for you.

Summer.

Then came bright Summer—we were *one:*
The stock dove cooed, from many a stately tree;
Each flower stood listening in the noonday sun,
Unvisited by humming bird or bee—
Chained by the loving songs, I sang to Thee.

Autumn.

Then came brown Autumn; and her faded leaves
Were quivering to the blast, or haply strewn
On melancholy graves. Her rustling sheaves,
And chirping insects—mournful e'en at noon—
Gave, to my harp, its melancholy tune.

Winter.

'Tis now dread Winter clad in shroud of snow;
Yon kneeling snow-bird asks a paltry meal,
In isolated chirpings, sad and low,
Making to Heaven his last appeal:
So chirps my harp; and so to Heaven I kneel!

PRELUDE.

Spring—with its Vernal Constellations and prophecies to Parthenon.

Earth, at this season, enters Virgo, which leads and interprets the minor galaxies, Libra, Scorpio and Sagittarius.

Flying around the Sun, thro' boundless space,
Earth sees him more intent upon her face,
Blushes in beauty, and displays her charms,
While Virgo's jewels flash upon her arms;
Prolific *Vines* and *Corn*, to heaven they lift,*
Prophetical of sacramental gift.
She whispers to the panting Earth : "Beware!
" Your safety lies in sacrament and prayer.
" Remember how, when yet the world was young,
" E'er prophet spake, or raptured minstrel sung.
" Noah came forth, from God's own brightness, blind,†
" And gave the Zodiac, to teach mankind.
" Leo, the mighty, and the Virgin true,
" Were given by heaven—Themselves a heaven for you !

" Chaldean Shepherd, and Egyptian King,
" Beheld me gazing on enraptured Spring,
" Like Iris changing—changing but the *name*,
" My benefactions ever more the same.

---

*The figure of Isis was adored by the Egyptians in this constellation, who represented her as carrying *branches* and *corn* in her arms. Even the Chinese Zodiac preserves the *yellow corn*.

†Mentem nostram non minus caligare ad Divina, quam oculos noctuae ad lumen Solis.

Grotius *de veritate*, p. 181, annol : (b) supported by Aristotle's Metaphysicorum —II chap-1.

"Now Thetis, then Aphrodite awhile,
"All Heaven and Earth rejoicing in my smile.
"Pallas Athene;—Parthenon sublime
"And Iris rose upon the wings of time;
"Chaldean first beheld her wings unfurled,
"With seven colors shining on the world—

"What means that rainbow? Who those colors gave?—
"Seven sacraments to light the very grave!*
"Chaldean Shepherds o'er the mountains trod,
"Saluted Mary and adored their God!
"Tho' new the name—all men had worshiped me,
"The light of earth, and glory of the sea—
"A Virgin blessed with heaven's own purity!

"Devils might counterfeit my form in part,
"But still this image rested on the heart;
"Honored throughout the world one sacred name,
"Till Luther fell, and lustful Henry came.
"See Scorpio, bent into a garland great,
"As if to crown the universe with crime,
"While his huge claws assail thy very gate,
"O Justice! looking down from heaven sublime,
"They clutch at stars, and climb the very skies,
"But Pan Electric's thunders blast them as they rise.

"Lo, Sagitarius, on another side,
"Assails the scorpion, with his bended bow,†

---

*Sapientia ædificavit sibi domum, excidit *columnis septem*. * * * * Miscuit vinum, et proposuit mensam suam. Misit ancillias suas ut vocarent ad arcem (*columnis septem*) et ad mœnia civitatis: * * * * Venite, comedite *panem* moum, et bibite vinum quod miscuit vobis. In festis B. M. V.

†Arcum conteret, et confringet arma; et Scuta comburet igni.

11

"For Truth and Justice ever more preside,
"Tho' tender mercies from my bosom flow,
"Till myriad constellations lost in one
"Shall shine forever—God's anointed Son!"

PARTHENON—PART I.

Spring.

Now the red maple kisses the blue skye,
Peach blossoms scent the river, and the shore;
Ten thousand beauties break upon the eye,
And the bluebird builds her cottage at my door;
Her songs of sweetness emulating mine,
To "Home, sweet home," and Parthenon divine.

All nature smiles, but April showers, soon
May cloud her beauty; or returning night
Snatch it from Parthenon; but the sweet moon
Shall fill yon valley with a flood of light;
And the stars sing on, as they were singing here,*
When Eve was beautiful and Earth without a tear!

Then pause a moment, and attend my song.
O, ever changing Nature—sad or bright—
My own capricious Beauty! how I long
To clasp thee with a lover's fond delight;
To hold thee with a Seraph's pure embrace,
And gaze forever on thy matchless face!

Now in sweet sunshine, now in clouds—Ah me!
With roses on thy bosom, or a crown of thorn,
Thou art more than beautiful; and must be
My heart's own idol, noon, and night, and morn,

---
*"And the morning stars sang together for joy!"

Till close these eyes forever, then in tears,
Behold me, listening to the music of thy spheres.*

We met this morning, when thy robe of green,
Resplendent with its dew drops (fairer far
Than tawdry diamonds) scarcely could be seen,
For shadows waiting on the morning Star,
That crowned my Beautiful; but vanished soon,
When thou didst put aside thy crescent moon.

That crown and crescent, gently laid aside,
Ten thousand songsters with enraptured strain,
Salute their Queen—Heaven's own Mysterious Bride!*
And the whole world is beautiful again.
For Mary—like, from Bethlehem, you greet,
Wise men, with incense, falling at your feet.

In every land, from western mountain wild,
To gorgeous City and the storiéd East,
Wise men, with offerings to the Holy Child,
Invite the Pilgrim to a heavenly feast;

---

*The doctrine of celestial harmony, was common to all the nations of the East. To this divine music Euripides alludes:—" Thee I invoke thou self-created Being, who gave birth to Nature, and whom light and darkness, and the whole train of globes encircle with eternal music."

> Look, how the floor of heaven
> Is thick inlaid with patines of bright gold;
> There's not the smallest orb, which thou behold'st,
> But in his motion like an angel sings,
> Still quiring to the young eyed cherubim;
> Such harmony is in immortal souls;
> But, whilst this muddy vesture of decay
> Doth grossly close it in, we cannot hear it.
> *Shakespeare.*

While Nature brings, tho' fallen once with man,
The tears and spices of a Magdalen.*

Nor these alone; as well my humble cot,
O, Nature, and its inmates kneel with Thee;
Thy beauty hovering o'er each hallowèd spot,
In sunshine and in shower, each vine and tree,
The verdant lawn, encircled by yon blue
Eternal Mountains, kneel to Heaven with you.

Here gentle lovers wander, sigh and talk,
Followed by roses, with as tender sighs;
Sweet daffodils enamel every walk,
And violets look up, with soft blue eyes;
While gushes from the ground a fragrant flood,
O, Hyacinthus, in thy purple blood!

That blood, sweet boy—Parthena's sacred art,
Apollo bright, and Hercules the strong, .
Diana's bow, and even Cupid's dart,
What are they now? an ill-remembered song—
Gone with the warrior and his broken hilt—
Scarce echoed by the temples to them built!

And so must pass my Parthenon, with time;
These scenes of beauty all be marred; but then
ETERNAL TRUTH built in lofty rhyme,
Thro' broken columns, and the homes of men,
Shall still resound; and every cadence sweet
O, Parthenon, bring homage to thy feet.

---

*"The whole creation groaneth, and travaileth together until now." (St. Paul.) "All *nature* felt the wound." (Paradise Lost.)

Sweet honeysuckles, to the breezes bend,
With boughs and bees, above my humble thatch;
While merry voices, with their murmurs blend,
And morning sings for joy. O let me catch
A glimpse of angels, passing to thy view,
And dwell sweet Nature, evermore with you!

Here let me dwell, on Parthenon with her,
Whom ancient wisdom pictured *pure* and *wise;*
Fell at her maiden feet, a worshiper,
And built great temples, 'til they touched the skies
Parthena heit, but now an empty name,
Except that Parthenon preserves her fame.*

Yon blue horizon, with cerulean wall,
Of lovely mountains, holding in their arms
Manors of olden time; but more than all,
Their memories, exalt thy matchless charms,
Become, O Parthenon! a part of thee,
And live forever in thy minstrelsy.

Yon capitol, with battlements that loom,
Like a lone city wedded to the skye:
Now gazes on Mount Vernon's lonely tomb,
And pays to Washington a pensive sigh;
Then turns to Parthenon, with smile as bright
As the gay sunbeam dancing on its height!

Thro' yonder gorges blue, more distant hills,
Like monarch ironclads along the deep,

---

*The *name* may perish but man's ideal of Isis, Aphrodite and Parthena, must live on while the soul of man survives. Not only *Wisdom*, but *immaculate purity* is expressed in this very word Aphrodite.

May heave volcanic fires, if Nature wills,
Or like an infant on her bosom sleep—
O, scenes of beauty, lift your heads and sing,
My household angels beautiful as spring!

JEWELS OF PARTHENON.

Ah, lovely Leila—fading but more dear,
Like pensive Autumn, with her hectic shades
Crowned with glories of the parting year—
Each floweret fading—lovelier as it fades,
O, far more beautiful than morning's glow,
Yon shadows lengthening in the vale below!

Those lengthening shadows, where the streamlets leap,
Are lovelier for the streams so crystal bright,
More beautiful where yonder roses sleep,
Eternal Morn upon the lap of Night!
Those streams and roses but the counterpart
Of your own loveliness, ye treasures of my heart!

How oft, in yonder portico, at eve,
Like angels' wings, its arches bending o'er,
With songs of merriment your bosoms heave,
Or tears salute some memory of yore!
Then roused again, from transient tears or sighs,
Ye light the hour, with laughter as it flies.

O, songs divine! O, beauty singing there!
Never did miser, more his treasures bless,
Tremble to touch, or feel them half so dear,
As my full heart, this world of loveliness!

And can it be, that frosty wind may sweep,
My flowers from Parthenon, to yonder steep!

Again they sing—now deep and solemn strain!
"*Sweet home*" perchance, or plaintive "*auld lang syne*"
Now classic melody, or deep refrain,
From Handel, Fauvre, or Reubenstein—
Swelling to Heaven, so beautiful and sweet,
That unseen angels linger at their feet!

Bending with Franklin, gazing on a spark,
Genius sublime, but unpretending; see!
Or rather wisdom, soaring with the lark,
Thro' all the regions of Philosophy,
Where technic halls, with many a queer device,
Learning, and wit, from every land entice.

But fly, my harp, sublimity; and sleep,
While vulgar doggerels to the banjo sing,
Another subject from Perdition's deep,
Offers a respite to thy lofty string,
Let meaner objects shuffle for a while—
Unworthy Genius or his gentle smile!

Lately yon senate in a venal rage,*
Crawled at his wingéd feet, to gather muck,
Became the by-word of a laughing age,
And gave a world of merriment to "*Puck*"—
He "girdled Earth, in forty seconds"—now,
Let Pan Electric Statesmen, tell us how?†

---

*Sacra fames auri. See Appendix. A, B.
†The Pan-Electric Company have, on their stock, an engraving of Puck, exclaiming, "*I girdle Earth in forty seconds.*"

In " forty seconds," they had pounced upon,
A *"world"* of genius,—girdled it around—
And maddened, by the seeming victory won,
Trampled their Benefactor to the ground;
But springing up, he only telegraphed—
Touched them with lightning, and the whole world laughed!

A great guffaw, burst forth from *Uncle Sam,*
Echoed by all from Mexico to Maine,
Cleveland's great jelly, shook into a jam;
And rapture lighted up the face of Blaine.
The lightning ceased—Its author let them go,
Pitied alike, by laughing friend, and foe.

But now in yonder halls, serene as spring,
He weaves the lightning to a wreath of flowers:
Or labor finished, where the linnet sings,
Wanders with Beauty to her fairest bowers—
Dove-like in peace, but terrible in wrath,
If Young assail, or Garland cross his path!

But Parthenon, despite the Statesman's craft
Shall flow thro' ages, bearing them along;
Ages shall laugh, as first a nation laughed,
To see them whirling on the tide of song:
There shall they live, like ripplets on a river—
Like flies in amber,* let them live forever!

Return my harp to Parthenon, and sing
Manhoods own Kohinoors, in yonder throng;

---

*ELECTRON—Electricity was first discovered in Amber; from the Greek of which substance, its name was derived; long before Lysander, another statesman, " *eked out the lion's skin, with the foxes!"*

To dashing chivalry, your honors bring,
For youth and valor listen to the song:
There do they stand; to home and heaven true,
Their souls as lofty as yon mountains blue!

Bridget and Barney lowliest in the rounds
Of Jacob's ladder reaching to the skies,
Now herd my flocks, or linger on the grounds,
And find a heaven in each others eyes—
Their love as true, without the pomp of wealth,
Their riches *Honor*, *Purity* and *Health*.

Such dower was thine, O, guardian of my home,
Mysterious Mary, ever young and fair!
Mightier than all the muniments of Rome,
And yet a gentle mother smiling there.
Of fallen empires—ruined worlds a part,
She comes to me, and breathes upon my heart—

Points to the flowers, blooming at my feet,
To stars above me, looking down from Heaven.
Then to my "jewels;" and in accent sweet:
"Dost know for what?—by whom such joys were given?
Start not immortal! they were given by me—
Handmaid of heaven from Eternity!"*

And oft recounting such mysterious words,
I seek companionship with vulgar men,
Who fly away, like shallow pated birds,
Laugh at my dreams, and pity me—but then,

---

*Uno modo in Seipso. Secundum quo l jam in actu est. Et sic non considera-
tur ut futurum, Sed ut praesens. (St. Thomas quaestio xiv, p. 131.)

She whispers soft: " *Theotokos*,* supreme,
Was God's eternal thought, and Heaven's awakening dream!

Then points to Egypt, once her mystic home,
Whose pyramids but mock the dead within,
To lost Persepolis and Ancient Rome,
As monuments of misery and sin.
But promises, while yonder sun toils on,
Humility and Faith to Parthenon!†

Last, but not least, yon owl‡ O, Parthenon,
Thy guest from Athens, at my very door!
'Tis a strange thing, but there she ponders on
Thy mysteries, and Parthenon of yore;
All day—all night—her temple in yon tree,
She offers up her lonely life to thee!

Never so strange a thing, that owlet came,
To gaze upon a cottage, night and day!
If bird or devil, syllable some name!
Art Thetis or Minerva, or but common clay?
Who sent thee hither? where thy temple now,
Changed for yon willow, and its hollow bough!

---

*Mother of God, in the Catholic creed was inserted to fence out, from the Church all Heretics, who denied that our Divine Lord's Divine Nature was born of the Blessed Virgin.—Prov. 9. & 31. & 10. Canticles, 24:24. Isa. 7:14-11, 1-19. 1. Luke 42:43. Matt. 2:13. John 19:25. Gen. 3: 15-24:17. Ps. 18:6-44 9 & 10, 41:56.

†Hoyt Nichol's fine poem, makes the Sun "*toil on*" without a Sabbath. Alas! how bleak the Poet's mountains! His soul, how desolate!

‡An owl makes her home in a hollow willow at the front door of Parthenon, and has grown so tame, that the children feed it—I have seized upon this circumstance to contrast paganism with christianity—so far as the owl, sacred to Minerva, suggests that all mankind, yearn for an immaculate Virgin-mother.

Didst gaze on Athens and her Parthenon,
When Socrates drank Hemlock; and, alas!
Looked up despairing to the very sun,
That lighted up Plataea and thy pass,
O grand Thermopolyæ; but gave mankind
Only a light that struck the nations blind!*

Didst hear his high philosophy? or Plato's song,
Discoursing with the stars, but all in vain?
O, tell me owl mysterious, how long
The nations slept! and shall they sleep again!
Say, where Minerva? Do the stars shine on?
Then where thy Goddess—Where her Parthenon!

Now the bright moon again comes up in gold,
Another Goddess, with a Virgin's mien:
And nature seems her very breath to hold,
Enraptured by the beauty of the scene;
But shedding tears, she cried: "unshriven owl!"
"Reveal the mystery of thy mournful scowl!"

When thus it answered: "now unsanctified,
" But 'ere the stars came forth, I dwelt in Heaven,
" And scowl to gaze upon yon ruin wide—
" My worship vanished, and my temples riven!
" For I was beautiful, at God's right hand,
" And weighed in balances, the sea and land!"†

---

*Aesculapius to whom Socrates offered up *a cock*, just before he drank the hemlock, was a son of Apollo—the Sun.
†Before the mountains were settled, before the hills was I *brought forth* and when he prepared the Heavens, I was there: Then I was by Him, as one brought up with him; and I was daily His delight.—Prov. Ch. viii, v. 25-30. Minerva had told this lie so long to the Athenians, that possibly she had come to believe it; but

"Cast out with Satan, for my wisdom's pride,
"Long did I lead the nations deeper down:
"My Parthenon was then Appolyon's pride;
"Glory of Athens, and her brightest crown!
"No heart have I to feel, but fully know,
"That *knowledge* can not lift us from below!

Then a soft whisper rustled through the wood:
"My name Minerva—nothing to yon Bride,
"Who gives to Heaven and Earth her precious blood,
"Flowing on Calvary, from Jehovah's side,
"Weep not O, nature! Heaven and Earth attest,
"And echo their loud cry *finitum est.*

"Yourself, as well, stood once at God's right hand,*
"Beheld the rising universe and smiled,
"Yon rolling ocean, and my measured land,
"Eve's vine—clad garden, and her woodland wild—
"But Calvary looming up thro' distant years,
"Obscured their brightness, and awoke thy tears.

"Eve but embodied, thee in figure dim, ;†
"Adam adored, and angels gazed upon—

---

she had only been a subordinate in Heaven; and not in any sense comparable to Her spoken of in the Mass and Offices of the Catholic Church, thus: Dominus possedit me in initio viarum suarum antequam quidquam faceret a principio. Ab æterno ordinata sum, et ex antiquis antequam terra fieret.

Nondum erant abyssi, et ego jam concepta eram; necdum fontes aquarum eruperant, necdum montes gravi mole, constiterant, ante colles ego parturiebar—*In Festis B. V. per annum.*

*Natura antem prior est quam intellectus; quia natura cujuscumque rei est essentia ejus. Question LX, Conclusio, Articulus 1.

Est antem hoc commune omni naturæ ut habeat aliquam *inclinationem*, quæ est *appetitus* naturalis vel amor; quæ tamen inclinatio diversimodi invenitur in diversis naturis, in *unaquacunque secundum modum ejus.*

†Praterea quod non creatum, non est creatura. Si igitur in his quæ sunt a

23

"Thou from thy God proceeding—Eve from him,
"But now their Paradise forever gone,
"Mary, thine own embodiment of grace,
"Gives, the lost world, a new and heavenly race!*

"A spotless virgin, to her God resigned,
"But all unconscious of her lofty state—
"O'ershadowed by *The Holy Ghost*, like wind
"On yon Baptismal font immaculate;
"Gives the *New Race*, as erst *The Holy Ghost*,
"Brooding o'er *Chaos*, yon celestial host.†

"She sat for ages on a snow-white throne—
"Built ere the stars came forth—at God's right hand;
"Built from Eternity, beside His own;
"And from it gazed upon "*The Promised Land*"—
"She his first thought (if first with Him could be),
"And Thou her morning dream—Herself in mystery?

"Each quickened soul, an arrow from the skies,
"Falls festering in the rotten flesh of Earth,
"But her's all purity, and great as wise,
"From God's own bosom struggled to its birth,

---

natura, non adjungatur creatio, sequitur quod ea quæ sunt a natura, non sunt creaturæ; *quod est hæreticum.*

Sed *contra* est, quod Augustinius (Super Gen) distinguit opus propagationis, quod est opus naturæ, ab opere creationis *Conclusio.* Creatio non admiscetur operibus *naturæ* et artis; sed aliquid ad illarum operationem præsupponitur. Quæstio XLV.

Uno modo in Seipso, secundum quod jam in actu est. Et Sic non consideratur ut *futurum*, sed ut *præsens.* St. Thomas questio XIV, P. 131.

*John 1:12-13. Eph. 1:19, 2:10. I Peter 1:3-23.

†John 3:3—Unus erat toto naturæ vultus in orbe; quem dixere chaos, rudis, indigestaque moles * * * * Sidera cœperunt toto effervescere cœlo. Ovid Met. II.

"And like yon flower, on Death's anointed head,
"Remained *Immaculate* among the Dead!

"Destined by Heaven to bruise the serpent's head,
"(Alas, poor Eve—her own sweet image there)—
"She walks the Earth, as one among the dead,
"Pure as her Holy Son, and passing fair—
"Her Beauty, Nature, God alone could see
"In his own bosom, prophesying Thee!*

"Lo, the sweet maiden on Judea's hill,
"Chosen to be the spotless Bride of God!
"God's holy Mother, suffering every ill—
"Chosen to bear the smiting and the rod—
"A sweet Redeemer of the lost and blind,
"Spotless as snow, but suffering for mankind!

"Her soul *Immaculate* thro' nature reigns—
"Inspires each miracle to bless the Earth,
"From promised sacrament, in yonder grain,
"To Vine clad mountain, and the floweret's birth!
"Her sweetest tints O, Nature given to thine,
"As God's own Love, and budding worlds combine! †

---

*From the *beginning*, and *before the world*, was I created; and unto the world to come, I shall not cease to be; and in the holy dwelling place, I have ministered before Him. And so was I in Jerusalem. And took root in an honorable people, and in the portion of my God, his inheritance; and my abode is in the full assembly of saints—Eccli. 24:6-16.

†And I, John, saw the New Jerusalem, the holy city, *coming down from God, out of Heaven*; prepared as a Bride, adorned for her husband—Apol. 21:2.

Even the Pagans had a dim idea of this heavenly love.

At ubi Spiritus *amore* principorum suorum tactus est. Grotius de veritate. Phœnicum Theologia.

25

"Behold thy kingdom, nature, thus enlarged,
"Thy grain and waters, grape and flowers to be,
"With a *new life*, and holier function charged.
"In the new kingdom given to Heaven and Thee;
"For Sacramental graces linger with them all—
"Redeemed with man—not angels—from the fall!

"No longer now shall sorrow till the ground,
"But Priests of nature cultivate the Earth;
"The plowman sees an Altar in each mound,
"In every flower a sacramental birth;
"While doubly blessed, Gods own anointed Priest,
"Brings nature's offering to the *Heavenly Feast!*

"Lo Abel kneeling, with his *corn* and *wine;*
"To make atonement for a brother's ire,
"The *Christ* prefigured in a *Priestly* line,
"Reaching from Eden, to the world on fire!*
"Exalted Nature, look abroad and see
"Yon rising nations—all compelled like thee!

"Their sacrifices evermore proclaim,
"The *Priesthood*, a *Necessity* of Time;
"In every offering to Jehovah's *name*,
"Wherever altars rise to Heaven sublime!
"Delusive Earth, and Heaven seem to meet,
"Ever pursued by Adam's bleeding feet!

"Lo the long line of Aaron robed in red—
"Yon gorgeous temple rising up to Heaven,

---

*From the rising to the going down of the sun my name shall be great among the Gentiles and in every place *Incense shall be offered unto my name.* Malach. 4; 11-12.

"What clouds of sacrifice! what slaughter dread!
"What thundered music till the skies are riven!
"'Tis but the prelude to yon wondrous thing—
"The sacrifice of Heaven's Eternal King!

"Yon watery deluge sweeping o'er the world;
"Yon lonely ark where boundless billows swell;
"Yon cloudy banners to the sky unfurled,
"And storms that terrify the powers of hell—
"Proclaim the wrath of Heaven, and yonder home—
"Thy bark St. Peter, and its anchor *Rome!**

"Behold yon patriarchs, gazing on the skies,
"Their flocks around them, thro' the silent night!
"What aspirations in their bosoms rise!
"What gleams of glory from yon mountain height—
"Obscure but dazzling—see, the darkened sun,
"And Heaven atoning for a world undone!

"Hark to yon earthquake, see the staggering hills:
"Lo, Mary struggling with her ancient foe;
"His hissing triumph, all creation fills,
"As his God cries out in agonizing woe—
"Now at her feet, the writhing serpent lies!
"For Jesus bows his bleeding head and dies!†

"With earth-quake tread, He now descends to Hell
"Behold the prophets, kneeling to his name,
"Who long to see, but more to hear him tell
"The mysteries of Redemption, and proclaim

---

*See Appendix C.
†The seed of *the Woman* shall bruise the serpent's head. (Genesis.)

" Their freedom promised—prophesied too long—
" Hark, the loud shout! The triumph of their song!*

" See far beneath them in eternal woe,
"Falling thro' sulph'rous clouds, those monster kings
" Whose sacrileges plunge them far below
" Earth's vilest sinners, and her meanest things—
" *Mene mene tekel upharsan,* all .
" Howl in despair, loud sobbing as they fall!

" From Persian Monarch, down to Catharine's foe—
" England's adulterous and bloated beast—
" Down to the false Immanuel, now "*Diabolo*"—
" See them descending—not to Persian feast—
" But ever cursing—falling—spit upon
" By fiery lightnings, naked and undone!

" Like worms all writhing—hiding with their hands—
" Not the vile nakedness they revelled in;
" But bloated faces, lest in other lands,
" They meet again some partner of their sin;
" Or suddenly, beyond the realms of grace—
" More horrid still—A Saviour's wounded face!

" You saints now burst the cerements of the tomb!
" Behold a thousand times ten thousand souls,
" Their King escorting—Hark the thunder's bomb!
" Now to the very gate of Heaven it rolls—
" Immanuel triumphs! up to Heaven He flies!
" Seraphic legions, guard Him to the skies!

*He preached to spirits in prison with Noah before the flood. (St. Peter Epis.)

"Yon Priesthood mock—unmoved by Mary's sigh,
"While Peter preaches to the multitude
"'Behold *The Rock!*—exultingly they cry—
"'The mighty Prince! with heavenly power endued!
"'And yonder *woman*—Blessèd to be known
"'*Throughout the world*, and Peter on a *throne!*'

"Lo all the Nations now at Peter's feet!
"That mystic *Rock* on which his Maker built;
"The lonely Fisherman, has mounted to thy seat,
"O, Constantine—his sword reversed—its hilt
"A holy Cross—*hoc signo*, in the skies,
"To which all nations turn their wondering eyes.

"Thy Queen, O, Constantine, at Mary's feet,
"Ages to come, salute her '*Queen of Heaven;*'
"Ave Maria! every where repeat,
"In thunderedmusic, till the skies are riven.
"Attila—Genseric, behold her now,
"And red Lepanto gazes on her brow!*

"Behold Columbus on the stormy deep!
"'*Santa maria,*'* thine, 'Christ-bearing dove!'†

---

*Maitland, Roscoe, Hallam, and all great Protestant writers on The Middle Ages, attribute European civilization to the Catholic Hierarchy: and, in its last great struggle, as the Crescent went down, upon the gulf of Lepanto, A. D. 1571, thousands assembled around the Vatican, were repeating the *Ave Maria*, when The Holy Pope, St. Pius V, in a celestial vision, saw the Crescent fall, and announced it to the multitude. Though the Jews mocked when an Angel prophesied Mary's enduring kingdom; and still more, when Our Divine Lord foretold Peter's power; though Protestants may still despise, and Infidels revile, *the facts of history remain!*

†Columbus' ship: but his name Christo-pher—Columbus, was given before he sailed to give our Divine Lord to America!

" Fly to the rescue, where yon millions weep,
" Strangers to Mary and a mother's love!
" Now Xavier journeys to the Pagan East,
" And calls her millions to the Heavenly feast!

"'Santa Maria!' "Xavier!"* ' *Christ-bearing dove!* '
" O why should Heaven, in name mysterious, shroud
" Her plans of mercy and her deeds of love!
" Like strategy in storm of battle loud,
" Mary beguiles the cunning of her foe,
" And wins the battle at a single blow!

" Wins East and West, with millions yet to come,
" Ten thousand millions, as the sun toils on,
" To recompense the losses of her home,
" Where faith once blossomed brighter than the sun;
" She sees the learning which her wisdom made,
" Striking her bosom with ungrateful blade.†

" Sees Europe fall away—an iron age
" Bent upon lucre madly rushing on;
" Burning with lust, bold devils, in their rage,
" Personify God's own Anointed Son!‡
" Perverting grace to every low desire—
" Heaven's wrath is kindled! lo, the world's on fire!

" Behold what clouds, on yonder mountain dread!
" 'Ten thousand lightnings from a wounded brow
" Reveal *Three Persons*, and a robe of red!
" The same we mocked on Calvary, but now

---
*Savior.
†See Appendix D.
‡Dramatis personæ! O, Anglesia, horresco referens!

"Its flaming grandeur lighting up the sky,
"Revolving planets melt, and suns before Him fly.

"Lo! at his feet another cloud as dread,
"Lurid its light, but yet revealing there,
"Mercy exhausted, with uplifted head,
"And wringing hands—her shrieks upon the air.
"A *Mother* pleading, as a *Mother* pleads—
"Her hands imploring, as her bosom bleeds.

"Ah! who could stand the terrors of that day?
"God's lightning wrath upon the Universe!
"No *Mother* there, no tenderness to stay!
"No bosom, once that angry judge's nurse.*
"Why cease those thunders?†—Millions saved by *One*,
"Pleading the merits of her ONLY SON!

"Yet witlings scorn, and even pious fools,
"Owning allegiance to her Holy Son,
"Despise the power of Mary, tho' she rules
"The Universe—All Heaven and Earth as one!
"Her progeny a new and heavenly race,
"Shining along the firmament of Grace!

"In this great truth, like germ in yonder bud,
"See wrapped another, palpable and sure,
"That SHE, from Heaven dispensing 'FLESH and BLOOD,'
"In sacramental mystery, must be PURE—
"'In Adam all died, but Mary was exempt,
"From every stain, as e'en the Pagan dreamt.

---

*"Ubera quae lactassent." Infestis. B. M. V.
†Donec pertranseat furor tuus. F. B. F. M.

"Ah, how we struggled in that ancient time,
"To choke thy voice, O Nature, but in vain;
"For men would listen to its song sublime,
"And worshipped motherhood in many a fane,
"Their temples rose to Heaven and counterfeited all,
"Yet lured them by a gentle mother's call.

"When Jesus suffered and the nations saw,
"A holier mother, beautiful and dear;
"They left our temples—overthrew thy Law,
"O, lost Jerusalem, and flew to her,
"Blesséd throughout the world her sacred name,
"Till Luther fell and lustful Henry came:

"Bright Thetis on a sea shell pure as brine,
"Isis in lotus, wafted o'er the Nile,
"Diana's virtue—e'en the sacred nine,
"And Ceres with her gifts, in yonder aisle—
"Were inspirations, Nature, given of thee,—
"Of God's *Immaculate*, a prophesy!

"Obscurely seen, sweet Mary, even then,
"(Best known in Heaven to her angels dear)—
"Was mirrored dimly, in the souls of men,
"Who yearned for pity, in a mothers' tear;
"Beheld the Queen of Heaven, at God's right hand,
"And worshipped Her in many a Pagan land!

"Man's holiest instinct, prompted by the love
"Of a pure mother's heart in every home,
"Yearned for a mother, guileless as the dove
"Even in Egypt, Persia, Greece, and Rome—

"From Isis, down to Mary undefiled,
"The worship grew, and every desert smiled!

"Not Venus of the Bacchanal, but she
"Borne from the Ocean, on a pearl-like shell,
"(Pure as the salt, each home's necessity)—
"Snatching the lustful from a fiery hell—
"And given to penitence, as God was given,*
"To vindicate the unity of Heaven!†

"For ere the stars came forth, or matter was,
"God from eternity surveyed them all;
"Saw thee, O Nature, and prescribed thy laws,
"(His lone companions in the Empyreal)
"Mary first blessed, and then created thee,
"Her counterpart in love and mystery!‡

"His angels next, with sparkling eyes—all flame,
"If heavenly love to fire we compare;
"For Mary gave to every one a name,
"Still visible upon each pinion there.
"'Mother!' they sighed, and kneeling at her feet,
"Sang the same song that all mankind repeat!

"Ave Maria! full of Grace,
"Above all spirits blest,
"O, let us gaze upon thy face,
"And in thy bosom rest.
"Our God his mercies now reveal,
"In raptures never known—

---
*(St. Paul Eph. Romans) and (1st Cor. 8, 5-6).
†Notwithstanding the vulgar notion that the Pagans were Polytheists, they all believed in one supreme deity, hence Homer: Theos Theon Kai anthropon.
‡Ecls. 24; 6-16. Apol. 21: 2—(See notes page 21.)

"The holy love our spirits feel
"Exalted to thy throne!

"Obscured by Glory, He must reign,
"Forever dimly shown,
"But all his love comes back again,
"Commingled with thine own;
"To Heaven and Thee, our praise be given,
"For God is Thine, and Thou art Heaven!"

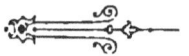

Thus sang the mystic bird, and Nature went,
Still weeping as she smiled—loved Mary most
Of all created dignities, and sent
Flowers to blossom for the Sacred Host,
With storms as well, to keep our woes in mind,
And all things beautiful to bless mankind.

With Mary, hand in hand, from mountain glen,
Down to the valley and sequestered dell,
She cheers and sanctifies the homes of men,
But most on Parthenon delights to dwell,
Where humble faith, in meekness clings to Her,
Thro' every change, a meek-eyed worshipper!

Vanished the owl—Minerva's better self—
Vanished her "quaint and half-forgotten lore;"
Down in the willow tree the little elf
Retired mysterious, and was seen no more;
But every night returns to gaze upon—
Perhaps to moralize on Parthenon!

For psychic wisdom—wisdom such as hers—
Objective Truth, without the light of Grace,
Can only mystify her worshippers,
And tho' she bring Minerva on her face,
To owl and bat yon darkened hole be given,
While Parthenon exalts her head to Heaven!

Here dwelt my fathers,* strangers all to pride—
The same sweet paths by generations trod;
In bold simplicity, they lived and died,
And soared thro' yonder arches to their God—
Fit consummation of a life well spent,
Remote from splendor, but with home content.

Their very slaves more happy here than when
Roaming in Congo, naked and accursed;
Their sweetest music from the Lion's den,
Their children brawny, but on brambles nursed,
O, better far, in yonder cabin bright,
To strike the banjo, and to dance at night!

Yon sword ancestral, hanging on the wall,
Still guards sublime, the battlements they built;
At Yorktown saw the British banner fall—
Saw them surrender many a golden hilt—
How flashed it then! what paths in battle made,
What lightnings sleep upon its rusty blade!

---

*Georgetown College, being my father's *Alma mater* and Baltimore his home; this anatopism might be excused without the "*licet Poetis et Oratoribus.*" At any rate, all the pictures here drawn of primitive simplicity, are strikingly true of "Long Meadows," and "The Haw Fields" of North Carolina, ten miles square of which were granted to the author's maternal ancestors; and in the old homestead their children lived, "right royally" until ruined by the late war. [See Wheeler's Reminiscences of *Orange County N. C.*

Ye days of old, what simple pastime yours;
What games of innocence upon the lawn;
When happy lovers fluttered from yon doors,
To gambol, o'er the grass, at early dawn;
At noon to slumber, or to plan anew,
The coming merriment, for hours that flew.

On dashing steeds, to scour the distant hills,
Maiden and Youth, all laughter as they flew,
To light as birds, by yonder murmuring rills,
For the wild strawberry, trembling in the dew,
Or gather chestnuts, falling fast around;
Where flowers invite, and plenty strews the ground.

Hark, to the foxhound! now the yelling pack!
Pellmell the lovers mount—go dashing on;
Sunshine or shower, or tempest black,
It matters not, they fly from Parthenon—
The fox is captured, and in circle sweet
They taunt the pirate trembling at their feet.

On flying steeds once more the lovers bend,
In headlong gallop, down to Riverdale;
To the wild scenes a merry laughter lend,—
Clear the broad ditch, or blooming hedges scale—
A Lord in homespun,* now a slave no more,
Receives them kindly—welcomes to the door.

---

*In Wheeler's "reminiscences of N. C." Col. Sheppard, of Long Meadows, is represented as wearing *homespun* manufactured by his own negroes—a striking contrast with his coach and four! but thus the fight commenced against *the Tariff* which brought on our civil war, and still agitates the country.

Fair Ladies, oft in London's gay saloon,
Give hearty welcome, to the family board,
Where dinner waits, without the golden spoon,
But better far, yon gardens' ample hoard,
With dainties—all unknown to Foreign shore,
Turkeys and Mallard captured at the door.

Fast fly the moments, merriment and song
Give wings to rapture, reigning now supreme;
The harp sings loud, and rebecs bear along
Ecstatic moments in a flying dream;
But happiness was never yet content,
In the gay lover, on his pleasures bent.

Mounting again, they dash the mountains o'er.
Rock Creek, thy valleys echo back the din,
'Til Kalorama* with its open door,
Invites to every luxury within;
And makes each guest forgetful for the while,
That his own delightful home had ceased to smile.

Here lies Decatur, keeping evermore,
The sword of Tunis buckled to his side;
No longer heedful of the tempest's roar,
Nor pirate's cannon, booming o'er the tide,
No longer mounts exultingly the wave,
But points to victory from a patriot's grave!

O, lovely Kalorama let me find
The pensive reed,† for which your name was given,

---

*Burial place of Commodore Decatur and residence of Barlow the Poet—where the author of "*Home Sweet Home*," was often entertained at a later day.
†Kalamos-oromai—not Kalos-orama.

And let its music sing to every wind,
Arrest yon stream, and stay the stars of heaven,
'Til coming ages pay their tribute here—
'Tis all Decatur asks—a Patriot's tear.

Here princely Corcoran opens far and wide,
Yon river park, where scenes of beauty glance.
Decatur smiles, his scabbard at his side,
Dreaming of Carthage, and her sons—perchance
Of modern Carthage, and her exile Payne—
Late homeward bound, but pulseless on the main.

Nor "*Home Sweet home*," nor Hail Columbia now,
The Poet's pallid lip may tremble o'er;
But Corcoran gazes on his pallid brow,
And lays him on a mother's lap once more,
That age on age, wherever "home" is "sweet"—
Their names may mingle, and their spirits meet.—

'Til Barlow's lyre, no longer tuned to Mars,*
Maecenas listening, and his Poet singing "home,"
Shall catch fresh music, from the fading stars,
And lead wherever happiness may roam—
Payne and Maecenas—Barlow leading on—
Like strains of music melting into one.

For every song that thrills a bosom here,
Is but a drop from Heaven running o'er,
And the great bard who wakes a pensive tear,
An unseen seraph, singing on that shore;

---

*The Columbiad was an Epic on the Revolutionary war.

Tho' deemed an exile as he seemed to roam,
His tuneful spirit called us to its HOME.

Not Payne alone—behold yon manor bright,*
Plumed with a castle in the olden time;
Thither ye lovers! and behold its light—
Another exile, and a soul sublime;
Gone is the Castle, and obscure the hill,
But rainbows linger on its summit still!

L'Enfant! L'Enfant! thy lonely grave is here;
Thy child, yon city, sees but knows it not:
For genius falls, without a sigh or tear,
His plans mysterious and his grave forgot;
Even till centuries have passed away,
When a cold world comes gazing on his clay.

Yon mazy streets, and capitol divine—
A Pantheon transported o'er the sea—
With all their dark significance are thine,
Singing a song to Liberty and Thee!
Freedom herself, exalted in yon dome—
Yon avenues to lead her children home!

Behold it there the glory of the land,
Lighting the generations yet to come:
O'er broken thrones and Tyrannies to stand,
Forevermore a beacon, and a home;
But thou L'Enfant, without a friendly stone,
Live in my song, thy monument and throne!

*See Exhibit O.

But why didst leave that dome so blank withal!
—Jeff Davis felt it—* placed a savage there—
A pagan goddess, but imperial,
With warlike feathers, for a virgin's hair;
O, tear it down! L'enfant, before his time;
Was dreaming of a symbol, more sublime:

Hast seen the Pantheon! St. Peter's dome?
L'enfant had seen them—All mankind shall see—
Do warlike feathers kiss the sky of Rome?
O, what, ye wise, is Christian liberty?
Yon Architect, unhonored in his grave,
Knew that The Cross—The Cross alone could save!

Milton and Shakespeare, for a hundred years,
Were all unknown—unknown the songs they sang,
But then awoke ten thousand sighs and tears,
Too late alas! to save them many a pang;
On—on my song, tho' twilight seems to die,
Her stars break forth, like blossoms on the sky!

Yon grand old manor, rich in memory's store,
L'Enfant upon her bosom, smiles a queen;
Cornelia-like, she asks for nothing more—
Her children are her jewels, and the green,

---

*Jeff Davis, when Secretary of War, felt that something was wanting to the dome, on which L'enfant would have placed a cross, but for intolerance:—Even the great Southern leader said in one of his speeches that Galileo, rose from the rack and cried out, "The Earth does move;" when all men of fair information know that Galileo was never punished thus, even for his impertinent and silly attack on the Bible, but perhaps the Orator was thinking of his own great countryman, *Jasper*, who stamped his foot on the ground, and cried out,
" *The Sun do move!*"

Neath yonder cedar, asks no vulgar tomb,
Where emeralds grow, and flowers immortal bloom!

He asks no tomb! But O, to guild your name,
To save your children, and yon city fair—
To snatch them from ingratitude and shame,
Go build, America, great arches there;
Like yonder dome to symbolize the free—
No honor to L'Enfant, but battlements for thee!

L'Enfant and Payne! behold yon Shepherd King:*
Forgotten where his pyramids arise;
See your own, SHEPHERD!—every honor bring,
And build a monument to touch the skies!
L'Enfant neglected, first your city gave,
SHEPHERD inspired her to wander to his grave!

Homeward again the lovers dash along;
The moon to light them and the stars to cheer;
The mocking bird enchants them with his song,
All earth is happiness and Heaven near!
Yon arch receives them, and in slumbers light,
They soon forget the rambles of the night.

Now for a sail! Mt. Vernon for the port,
Each lover climbs the dancing pinnace where,
Still linger traces of that ancient fort,†
Dear to the lover, for a flower there—

---

*The Shepherd Kings of Egypt built their own tombs—The Pyramids, that look down on more than 40 centuries.
†Running from Minnehaha springs through Parthenon grove. [See page 50.)

The wind is up—Mt. Vernon's princes wait,
With welcomes to the hospitable gate.

Yon city passed, their Mecca heaves in sight,
Virginia gives to Maryland her hand;
Custis and Lee, and Washington delight,
To waive them greeting—welcome to the land—
They climb the hill—Mt. Vernon bids them come,
Not only guests, but noblemen at home.

The prince of princes, dignified—serene,
Inspires with awe, unconscious of his power,
While gentle Martha, smiles a gracious queen,
And lends her beauty to the festal hour,
O, days of innocence, what graces then!
Our mothers *women*, and our fathers *men!*

No dude to flutter, and no painted face,
No sudden fortune lifting up the churl,
Nor venal politician dares to place,
His vulgar family in fashion's whirl;
But gentle manners—genius—worth adorn,
Exalted honor "to the manor born!"

No magnate smelling of the hangman's rope,
And incidents, that cronies blush to tell,
No trowsered woman lecturing the Pope—
Nor Garland, in a pan-electric Hell!
But Adams, Jay, and Jefferson sublime,
With modest women of the olden time!

No north-west Washington, was then sublime;
Sought by the vulgar, for the glint of gold,

Nor politician, crawling in his slime,
Consorted with the beautiful or bold.
But Bladensburg—yon eastern branch was then,
The Home of Honor, and shall be again!

Still lingering here, each scene of beauty cries:
" Come back, ye wanderers to the lovely plain—
" Fly from the vulgar, where yon mansions rise—
" The palaces of Cameron and Blaine—
" Your fathers call you, and with horrid hair,
" Rising again, rebuke your presence there!"

'Tis not the pomp of power, nor dashing plume,
And circumstance of war—nor mighty ships,
Nor squadrons charging to the cannon's boom,
Nor boundless plains and mountains from whose lips
Eternal Clouds repeat the battle's roar,
While mighty navys bristle on the shore—

They cannot make a people great—nor peace
Where luxury eats out a nation's heart,
And merriment and banquets never cease,
Till Freedom and her faithless children part;
But the brave men—pure women of a state,
These—*only* these—can make a nation great.

Back to Mount Vernon! to our lovers back!
Now murmuring waters bear them gaily on;
Fast flies the foam upon the pinnace-track;
And soon again they land at Parthenon:
To sleep again, impatient of the dawn,
And dreaming, kiss the blushes of the morn!

But let them slumber—leave them sleeping there,
Alas! they sleep forever on yon hill!
The flowers they planted, yet may bloom as fair;
Yon spring that welcomed, and its sparkling rill
May still sing on, and vulgar feet profane
The dust of heroes till they rise again:

Yet, not at Parthenon, for there no slave,
Barters his birth-right, for an Esau's mess,
But "on the native heath," McGregors brave,
Still walk abroad, in conscious manliness.
While gentle forms, in modesty sublime,
Reflect "our mothers" of the olden time!

If Avarice tempted, or for vulgar place,
Their hopes should quicken, or their bosoms burn,
Yon cloud-capped manor, and its kingly race,
Would check such folly, and to virtue turn:
For Lowndes is there—surveys each lowly glen,
Himself as modest, but the prince of men!

And near him, Goldsmith—Nature's finest mould,
Of generous manhood, living for mankind;
Alas, poor Vicar! could you see yon fold,
Tho' striped, and streakéd, as to Heaven they wind,
And hear St. Peter, calling them afar,
You, too, might follow, poor belated star!

My *quondam* self—with caul upon your face—
In conscious honesty you plod along;
But yet may hear, if worthy of such grace,
A Father's message, and a Mother's song:

When, unlike mine—(Her prodigal at best)—
Mary might give *your* gentler spirit rest!

Deserted village, sleeping at my feet,
Once, Bladensburg in military pride;
Where sable loungers linger on each street,
Indifferent to the Brave, or how they died;
Is yours yon field, where vines and clover wave
More mindful of the battle, and the Brave?*

The clover leaf—Its blossoms white, and red,
All intertwined, and trembling to the breeze
Like a wild harp, thrown down on Glory's bed,
Still answering to the murmur of the bees;
Its pensive music; and unbidden sighs,
Sweeter than incense, wafted to the skies!

Where now your Calverts, and the cavaliers
Who sprang to battle? Where the busy throng
Crowding yon mart† with anxious hopes and fears?
O, where the pomp of yonder Mansion‡ and the song
Of other days? Alas! departed all—
Yon dingy cabins now your funeral pall!

Fit retribution for the mournful scenes
Of yonder bridge—(another bridge of sighs)—§

---

*Battle of Bladensburg.
†Bladensburg, on the Eastern branch of the Potomac, was once a great Tobacco Mart—the rival of Baltimore.
‡The brick mansion built near the landing by Von Steers, the Antwerp Banker, who filled it with rare gems of art—is now the property of an old negro named Lee.
§Duelling ground.

Its glen detested, where the combat leans
On public sentiment, but Heaven defies;
What bloody drops have trickled there for years,
Alas! outnumbered by poor woman's tears!

Here the brave butchers Barron, Chilley, Graves,
And other statesmen, in a crimson pool,
Prove that the wretch who yields to—never braves
The Public—is a coward and a fool—
Egregious fool! who feared the mob and died—
At once a murderer and a suicide!

Alas, that genius, and exalted worth,
In evil hour should venture to such glen ;
And yet the noblest—bravest of the earth—
Purest of patriots and the best of men—
Decatur, Clay, and Hamilton sublime—
But let them pass; 'twas not a vulgar crime.

Cut in his stirrups, shining through, and through,
But red with rust, behold the name of Clay—*
We found them where he stood, with gauges true—
Better no witness had recalled that day—
But there we found them—there the very name,
That glitters on the pinnacle of fame.

See, on another side, his ashen staff,
Cut by his hand from Ashland long ago:

---

*The stirrups of Clay were lately dug up on the duelling grounds, his name in filagree work on the steps of each. How came they there? His massive goldhead cane, is also at Parthenon. The duel was fought at the Chain Bridge, Va.; but probably while Clay was practicing at Bladensburg, his horse took fright at the firing and lost his saddle. At any rate his stirrups are here.

There still the trees, the birds, the waters laugh,
Regardless of the hero lying low;
Whose relics here are treasured as a gem,
More glorious than a kingly diadem.

In Parthenon they greet the Pilgrim oft;
And oft Kentucky views each trophy there;
But where the form that mounted—towered aloft,
His plume of genius dashing on the air?
Immortal Clay, behold thy relics here,
And pay to Parthenon a grateful tear!

For she alone, in this degenerate age,
Defies yon Senate, and corruption's throng;
Records their follies, on a daring page;
And holds them dangling on the spear of song;
Suffers in poverty, to Ashland true,
And consecrates her friendless lyre to you!

Alas, for Bladensburg! in days of old
A race of monarchs, brighter than the day,
Bore thro' her wilderness a cross of gold,
And taught the simple savage how to pray.
Here first Religious Liberty was born,
Here first, alas! her altars overthrown?

From yonder springs, now Minnehaha hight,*
The weary savage slaked his thirst, and told

---

*<i>Minnehaha Springs</i> are on the river above Bladensburg, but on the lands of Parthenon. "The Little Spa" has been known for ages, but the Red and White Sulphur were unknown until the huge oak lying beside them tore away the bank in its fall.

What miracles were in the waters bright,
More precious than a universe of gold;
For here he knelt, and here the Jesuit stood
To bathe Minotti in a Saviour's blood.

O, Blood of Jesu! from the tree accursed,
Thro' holy waters still your currents flow:
And moved by heavenly benedictions burst,
In cataracts upon the sinner's brow.
Here knelt Minotti; while his spirit soared,
Higher than eagles to embrace his Lord.

Yon trees beheld him, and yon fallen oak,*
Stood sponsor with the chieftains all around;
It fell to earth, and healing waters broke
In torrents from the consecrated ground;
But still that fallen oak, neglected lies,
More eloquent than when it touched the skies!

So Washington majestic, sheltered here,
The wealth of empires hidden at his feet;
Yet there he lies, with scarce a grateful tear,
Mount Vernon's guest, without a winding sheet;
While Winter, to the fallen oak, still brings,
The robe in which he kissed a thousand springs.

That oak, through ages, watched the setting sun,
Its branches sang thy song, St. Salvadore,
Fresh from the Pinta, as the stars went on—
Had heard it chanted, on this very shore,
Where christian teachers, ere Columbus came,
Gave to the savage many a christian name!

*(See Appendix, M, N.)

Fountains of Youth!—(no fabled fountain now)—
Dispensed eternal life, and every wind,
Type of the spirit, kissed the savage brow,
Singing "*absolvo te*—thy gold refined,
" Live thou in faith, and purity, and truth,
"THIS IS THE FOUNTAIN OF ETERNAL YOUTH!"

Ponce de Leon! little did you know,
That blind Tradition, singing thro' the land,
Was but a christian minstrel sighing low;
The very harp that trembled in his hand,
Was snatched from Eric, when they laid him low,
Baptizing here a thousand years ago.*

That oak then rising; but a tiny bud,
Looked up to Heaven, and longed to kiss the sky,
Drank from the spring, and heard the noisy flood,
Of yonder river, madly rushing by
Like a great soul, above ambition's wars,
It rose to heaven, and dwelt among the stars!

That noisy flood (for never virtue strong
Rose scornful of the vile, but envy grew),
Marshalled its forces, in meanderings long:
And a great ocean on the monarch threw,
He groaned and fell, but leaping on the foe,
Sheltered the spring, still laughing on below.

---

*Before Columbus landed at St. Salvadore, the martyred Eric, from Greenland, had perished in America; and Ponce de Leon's "fountain of youth" was probably a tradition, which had wandered from Martha's vineyard—("vine yard")—to Florida.

So tortuous windings of the mighty clan,
Now striking Parthenon, in fearful ire,*
May raise her very battlements, and *Pan*
Dance on the ruins of her smouldering fire;
But Dagon's temple, tho' it kiss the sky,
Shall fall around her, ere those embers die!

Shall fall, a *by word*, on the shores of Time,
Immortal Truth beholding with a smile;
And Dagon's demigods, no more sublime,
Shall crawl with Pan, and many a satyr vile—
Like yonder streams, meandering as they go,
While love and beauty sparkle on below!

Oft have I seen Minotti wandering here:
A flaming cross, his bow and arrow now,
The moon-beam kissed it, and a glittering tear
Fell from the shadows of his lofty brow;
On yonder breastwork, straggling thro' the wood,†
Where once he fought, the spirit warrior stood!

"Too late! too late!" the mournful chieftain cried,
(And kneeling, kissed a flower at his feet:)
"'Twas here, alas! my Minnehaha died,
"This flower an offering from her bosom sweet,
"Unblessed of holy water, here she fell,
"To sleep forever in this lonely dell!"

Scarce had he spoken, when the flower stood,
Serene beside him, and with sighs as sweet.

---
*(See Appendix, A, B.)
†An old fortification, now overgrown with trees.

'Twas Minnehaha, still in maidenhood,
More beautiful than when she fell asleep.
"Weep not, Minotti," low the maiden sighed,
My dust is here, my spirit at your side.

That voice so sweet—never so sweet as now—
Startled the warrior and he would have fled;
But lo, a cross upon her radiant brow,
A crown of glory burning on her head!
"Weep not, Minotti," still the maiden sighed,
"'Tis better thus, than with a mortal bride.

"'Tis not too late, for ere my spirit fled,
"An angel touched the waters of yon spring;
"Flew to the wigwam, raised my drooping head,
"And scattered rainbows from his fiery wing:
"For thus can Mercy snatch the soul from Hell,
"And vindicate her sacrament as well."

Thus did she speak, and flames of living light
Burst from the Chieftain's melancholy heart,
Not earthly love, but God's own glory bright,
Blessing the soul as earthly loves depart.
There did she stand, in spotless maidenhood,
All bathed in splendor, lighting up the wood.

And ever since, when sorrow, grief or care
Cloud Parthenon, I wander to this wood,
To find the Chief, with Minnehaha there,
Surrounded by the beautiful and good—
Maiden and youth and warriors who reveal,
The buriéd past, and why yon waters heal.

Nor these alone, but many a wayward one—
Impetuous bards of every age and clime,
Whose mad'ning love had reason overthrown,
And hurled them from the battlements of time;
From penal fires they find a respite here;
But still lament with many a sigh and tear.

From yon embankment, guarding still the vale,
Garrisoned by many a poplar tall,
I once beheld the caravan, all pale,
As moving to a midnight carnival:
For some were cheerful, as in festal hall,
And robed in white, while others were more sad—
On one sat sorrow like a funeral pall—
This one now wept, and then again seemed glad,
While many a one, alas! with love and grief was mad.

Anacreon crowned with ivy, fresh and green,
That twined among his bays, inebriate seemed;
Laughing full merrily, and sang some Queen,
Forgot, alas! where once her beauty beamed:
Poor Dante* still of Beatricé dreamed;
Laura came sweeping by, as Petrarch sung,
Smiled at his tears, indifferent how they stream'd;
And poor Tasso, his wild hair backward flung,
Told in his eye, what woes his gentle bosom wrung.

---

*Il ecrive ces mots: Ici plus d'esperance.
      DELILLE.
—Lassat' ogni speranza.
      INFERNO, C. III.

Onward they move, a mighty host like these,
And many a one, alas! to fame unknown;
Poets who scorned a vulgar world to please,
But lived and died their sorrows all their own;
And as they moved, with many a sigh and groan,
Torquato wept, alas! he knew not why,
Saw vanishing the phantoms, one by one,
Lifted, to heaven, his overflowing eye,
And prayed for death as tho' 'twere some relief to die.

View them with scorn, ye cold, ungenerous few,
Whose hearts have never known love's sacred flame,
No hallowéd transports are reserved for you—
No niche of glory in the hall of fame;
The miser's meanness, and the villain's shame
May yet be yours, and children of your lust—
Poor brutes of passion—bastards, but in name,
Shall be no pledge of virtuous Beauty's trust,
Nor rise like flowers around to consecrate her dust.

What nerves the patriot's arm, the scholar's mind?
Or wakes to ecstasy the living lyre?
What name could thrill, with holy memories twined—
Wafting sweet incense to angelic choir;
If lost Luigia,* lovely Leonore†

---

*Veggio co 'bei vostri occhi un dolce lume.
ANGELO, sonnetto xii.

†———— E le mie rime ....
Che son vili e neglette, se non quanto,
Costei LEONORA co'l bel nome santo.
TORQUATO.

And one now living,* and whose smiles inspire
(Pleiads that rose to shine on every shore)
Were blotted out, with Love's celestial fire?
The bloom of Earth would fade, and Virtue's self expire.

GREAT STATESMEN.

Next came great statesmen, of the olden time:
Cloud covered Webster, dreaming of the sun,
Stood crying out in attitude sublime;
" May your last lingering glance thro' victories won;
" Behold yon banner, still on every shore!
" Union and Liberty forevermore!"

Then Clay pacific, pointing to yon wall,
Whose battlements a tale of ruin tell,
Cried out exultingly—" In yonder Hall,
We signed "*the Compromise*,"† and slavery fell.
For my whole life was sacrificed to gain,
Freedom to labor; from oppression's chain.

Here let me stand—like Moses on the mount,
My Country! O, my Country!! to behold
Thy rising centuries! O who can count
Yon gleaming stripes, and stars of burning gold?
Unconquered banner, tho' all ages rise,
And kiss the last star that rushes from the skies!

---

*LEILA, with Laura live!
Such fading plume from fancy's wing
Is all I have to give.
†Lord Baltimore's Mansion, now in ruins, was once a favorite resort for politicians. The Missouri Compromise was signed in its east wing.

Mighty Pacific how your curling crest
Kneels to her Majesty, from pole to pole!
Ye golden Islands, sparkling in the west,
Chained at her feet where conquered billows roll,
And thou Atlantic—all ye nations kneel,
To the same banner, with the joy I feel!"

Calhoun looked up—for crouching by the way,
He gathered up the fragments of a scroll—
Looked up imploringly and seemed to say:
"Are these your witnesses!—this parchment old?
'Twas once a bulwark riding o'er the sea;
LICENSE your name—Its name was LIBERTY."

And all around him, kneeling at his feet,
Were wounded soldiers—women sobbing loud,
And crying out: "Thou wonderful and great—
Unheeded Prophet of the coming cloud,
Behold our Country—Anarchy supreme!
George in the van, and liberty a dream!"

Next Wirt the orator, sublime but sad,
Points to yon shed where many a coffin sighs,*
And thus recalled his home: "My childhood glad,
Leaped from yon sill to gaze upon the skies;
And where the Sexton plies his mournful craft,
My cradle rocked—The stars looked in and laughed.

"O, where my kindred, and the blazing fire?
The merry jest that mingled with its blaze?

---

*William Wirt was born in the house where Mr. Gash carries on the undertaking business.

My gentle mother, and indulgent sire?
Friend and companion of those peaceful days?
My feet went forth upon a boundless sea—
Alas! the world! the world! its misery!"

Then Hamilton with gory locks, and Burr,
And Blanerhasset with his lovely bride;
While mounted devils pressing in the spur,
Went vaulting—leaping over them and cried:
"Genius and knowledge, follow us to learn
Your nothingness, where yonder fires burn."

Thus did a thousand times ten thousand weep,
'Til chanticleer proclaimed the coming day,
When suddenly, some flew from steep to steep,
To kiss the morning, on her bridal way,
For heaven is light, and hopeful spirits fly,
To catch a glimpse of Mary in the sky.

While guiltier things, if such still lingered here;
Poor prodigals, without a ray of hope—
Flew from the morning, to a covert near,
Where murder stalks, and politicians grope.
Chiefly yon ruins hide them from the light,
Once radiant with love and beauty bright.

Shine on ye stars, or rather take your veil,
For yonder comes the glorious king of day,
Symbol of God, exalted brightness hail;
Yon moon and stars with hidden faces pray,
And myriad altars, burning as they rise,
Send up their love and incense to the skies!

Vistas of glory come with dawning light—
Historic manors blooming all around;
Yon Capitol, with dome and banner bright,
Sits like a dew-drop on the grassy ground;
But O, what thunderbolts are sleeping there
At Freedom's call to leap upon the air!

Banner of beauty springing up from fire,
O'er fallen cities, smouldering around,
Rise like the phoenix, and my harp inspire!
Louder the music! Heaven and Earth resound!
Thunder thy battles! Let thine eagle soar,
And bear his thunderbolts to every shore!

Mt. Vernon—Arlington—yon dome attest,
Now looking up to Parthenon, and thee,
That North, and South—the mighty East and West,
Wherever billows roll or mortals be;
If once "CONFEDERATE" and to "UNION" given,
Must stand united, like the stars in Heaven!

RIVERDALE.*

Hail seat of Princes, mournful Riverdale;
Thy broken arches, and each barren dell—
Yon river, now without a bark or sail,
Thy fallen chapel, and its silent bell;
Repeat the story told a thousand times,
An epic sad—a song without its rhymes.

Lord Baltimore's Manor, adjoining Parthenon on the North.

Oh, where, Lord Baltimore, thy dreams? All fled?
Is yours yon mansion? Where its princely style?
Are all your gallants sleeping with the dead?
Your ladies bright—is not one left to smile?
E'en infancy that blossomed at your side,
Old age consumed—it withered here and died.

Yon ruins, and the graveyard, standing all
In solemn sadness, and the hoary trees—
The mildew, and the weeds upon the wall;
Could they but sing your sorrows; every breeze
Would wake you broken harp and waft the while,
Another story from Calypso's isle!

These scenes like her's, but once surpassing far—
Perfume, and flowers, and merriment and song;
Learning and wit, and beauty, like a star;
Leading the dance, and lighting it along!
Be still my harp, or sing in accents low,
Such weird strain, as only ruins know.

Yon stately hall fast crumbling to the dust,
In mournful silence, soon must follow him,
Whose portrait eere, and melancholy bust,
Lend awful sadness to the twilight dim—
Her pensive sighs, and shadows on the wall,
Not his alone—but offered for us all.

Each home of Peace, with Beauty's loving smile,
And every dream of happiness below;
Are given, but a moment to beguile
Our spirits from inevitable woe—

Fortune and Fame, the beautiful and brave,
But monitors that point us to the grave!

The Bard and Lyre—The soldier and his steed
Must all be heaped together with the dust
Of pagan warriors—men of every creed—
No record, to recall them—not a bust,
Tho' yonder sun—still gazing on the scene,
Reveals alas! the nothing they had been.

"*God's acre*" here, is more than grandeur needs,
A bit of Earth from all his vast domain,
To circumscribe his wants, while yonder weeds
More than supply his waving fields of grain;
They grow upon his bosom, as it fell;
And feed upon the dust he loved so well.

Yon mournful tablets, and the tales they bear
Thro' stormy winter, and the laughing spring;
Can never wake a sleeping bosom there,
Revive one hope, nor teach a heart to sing!
In cold obstruction they are doomed to rot,
By friends forsaken, and by foes forgot!

For who can snatch one trophy from the Grave,
Recall the soul or animate the dead!
Nature herself too impotent to save—
To move one heart, or lift a fallen head;
But God who made them—mighty now as then,
Breathes upon dust—behold it lives again!

Beneath yon stone a nobleman is laid,
Who fled from bigotry to freedom's home;
In yonder sky, his bannered cross displayed,
With hope as lofty, as its Heavenly dome;
Alas! the sun of liberty had set,
And Freedom's "Dove"* was only wandering yet!

For Bigotry pursued, and *Maryland*—
First to proclaim upon her virgin sod,
Welcome to all—to all a helping hand,
A peaceful home, and altars to their God;
Was first to fall, and Riverdale to save
A mess of pottage, owned herself a slave.

Worse than a slave, for to a Tyrant's freak,
She casts aside the Beautiful and True;
And O, for what? thy plaines, O Chesapeake?
Thy hills that climb to yonder mountains blue!
Alas! what ashes in their palms remain—
One sandy hill from all the vast domain—

That sandy hill, the heritage of all—
A mess of pottage for each hungry soul,
While winged Death keeps up his carnival
With Lords, and Ladies in yon dismal hole:
One sandy hill? 'Tis but a bit of earth,
Where yonder tombs commemorate their birth!

But let them sleep, the faithful and the weak;
Nor thou Presumption, with intolerant gaze,

---

*Lord Baltimore's ships were the "Dove," and the "Ark."

Revive their faults—sweet charity may speak
Of all they suffered—all they hoped; and raise
A mantle from her loveliness to fall,
And cover up the weakness of us all!

For many a noble heart, and generous hands,
Whate'er their faults, repose in yonder graves,
In vain spread out their ever-blooming lands,
O, vainer still their multitude of slaves!
There let them sleep; with every fault forgot—
All chained together in one lonely spot—

Lo, on another side, where many a slave
Went down from bondage; to a refuge dear,
Not e'en a shroud, to bind him in the grave;
Only one Master to awake him here—
A life of sorrow, and a death of pain;
The grave and rottenness—not rise again?

Here sleep the sturdy arms, and willing hands,
That toiled thro' life, for grandeur and repose;
To build yon mansion, turn the stubborn lands,
And make the manor blossom as the rose;
Here each may rest, no longer now a slave—
Tho' crowned with thorns—the thistle on his grave.

No marble bust, nor urn, nor statue here,
Not e'en a tablet, nor a line to tell
How faith and duty, linked with grief and fear,
Toiled for a master, and unhonored fell—
Not e'en "th'unlettered muse," a vine to wreathe,
Or o'er yon thistle, in her anguish breathe.

There let them sleep—The thistle flower blue—
Tear-eyed and beautiful, despite the thorn;
Looks up to Heaven, with a faith as true,
As yonder lily "to the manor born;"
For "thistle danger" oft to valor bears
"The flower of safety," if it bravely dares!

And he who falls unnoticed, and unknown;
No record to recount his patient toil;
Whether in battle, to the tempest blown,
Or sunk with brutes, that helped him till the soil.
If Truth, and Faith, and Fortitude prevail,
He needs no monument, to tell the tale.

Neath yonder thistle sleeps a sooty breast;
That gave its willing currents to a Lord;
Tho' dark* the bosom which his roses pressed
The stream that flowed, was whiter than a curd,
And the kind heart, that loved each tiny limb,
Nursed by the same fires, that nature gave to him.

Without a slab—low sunken in the grass,
Her grave neglected, asks a bit of sod,
Behold its desolation ye who pass,
But see her spirit, with your Mother's God;
Bewail your fault, and for your children weep,
Or write upon their tombs, "*Eternal sleep!*"

Yet who shall say that, in revolving years,
No blessings come, from sorrows suffered here?—

---

*"Black-Mamy" was the fond name, given to many a colored foster-mother.

That rainbows never spring, from falling tears,
Nor flowers from vine, where only thorns appear:
That yonder plant, which stands in stately gloom,
Shall frown a hundred years, but never bloom!

Pilgrims uncanonized, and yet sublime,
True to their God, and loving him supreme;
Without a footprint on the shores of Time,
Here sleep forever—but if spirits dream,
May clasp the children on their bosoms nursed,
And bless the very shackles they had cursed.

The conquering Chief, with palm upon his brow,
The Cavalier, and soldier Prince and Boor;
All in one valley! What avails it now,
That one was mighty, or another poor?
Each spirit bears its record to the skies,
'Tis there alone that virtue wins the prize.

HAPPINESS ATTAINED ONLY THROUGH SUFFERING.

Then let us dwell with innocence alone,
In conscious greatness for the grief we know;
Whose shadowy mantle; covers every one;
And promises protection as we go.
For *Grief* our mother dare not leave her child
Wandering alone upon the mountains wild!

Tho' dark her visage—tho' her tears fall fast,
She clasps us to her bosom, more and more;
O, swarthy bosom, will your currents last,
'Til my deep cup of misery runs o'er?—

Even in death, you hold us to your heart:
Children, from whom you cannot—will not part.

The brute you love not—never clasped the stars,
The flowers are laughing, and the landscape bright,
Only for man come up incessant wars
Delusive hope—its pang—affection's blight—
Yon tombs attest—yon ruins all his own,
And grief undying clings to man alone.

In every track he makes from Eden—see!
What bloody drops! What horrid thorns appear!
From hopeful youth, to age declining, he
But digs his grave—his shroud and coffin near!
Bear up immortal, bravely if you can,
For sorrow proves the dignity of Man!

Our Saviour's anguish and the tears He shed,
The woes of all around us cry aloud;
Point to the silent chambers of the dead;
And sorrow stands to cover with a shroud;
Then up to duty—do the work of Time,
And conscious Truth, will make our lives sublime.

Down with repining; Darkness comes apace,
Each life is short, behold the work to do,
Turn to the tempest, with a flint-like face.
Onward to duty—Faith can carry thro'—
And falling bravely, leave your tracks to tell,
To coming Valor, how a brother fell!

Ye sable monuments—my lyre unstrung,
Now let me leave upon a lonely grave;

Not o'er a Lord—for adulation sung;
But where yon grass, and thorny thistles wave:
For Her, who nursed my childhood, let it sigh,
'Til dews of pity tremble from the sky.

Again to Parthenon! as sailors long
Imprisoned on the deep, return once more,
To climb the mountain homeward, so my song
Greets Parthenon—her river and its shore,
Each walk meandering, and the quiet grove,
Where Duty wanders, hand in hand with Love!

Thus did they walk an hundred years ago,
When Virtue built in unpretending style,
Yon modest mansion, with its ceilings low,
Spanned by the portico whose sunny smile,
Gives welcome still, but when a cloud goes by,
Seems to admonish, and to breathe a sigh!

Gone the peach-blossoms, and the maple red,
For Spring is melting into Summer's arms,
But ere she weds him, and with drooping head,
Surrenders all the sweetness of her charms,
Her lingering songs, and fading flowers invite,
To the gay grove, and rivulet as bright.

And now yon city pours its reeking throng,
More numerous than locusts to the groves;
Yon woods resound with Bacchanalian song,
Where gallants wander with their many loves:
Exalted Nature, won at last by thee,
They spurn the palace for the spreading tree.

Beneath its ample boughs, in peace sublime,
Oft do I listen to the tinkling bells:
The browsing herd, and waters, till the chime
Of melting melody to heaven swells.
While warmer suns, now burning on each tree,
Leave the cool shade, to Happiness and me.

O, gorgeous wealth, and thou insatiate Prince,
Of Merchant Princes, sweltering in the town;
Why peril everything for lucre, since
You cannot emulate the poorest clown,
In happiness, nor drink from costly thing,
Water more cooling than his mountain spring!

What though the sources of your faucet teem,
With fish polluted, and the muck-eyed worm,
Sloughed off from carcasses, on yonder stream—
An epidemic hid in every germ—
Your thirst for gold, demands an ocean's swell,
Yon tiny spring can quench his thirst as well.

Compare your palace with my lowly cot,
Your tap'stered halls, with yonder beachen plank,
The broad blue sky, the clouds—forget it not—
Were never given to wretchedness and rank;
But to brave souls, to Earth and Heaven true,
Their cup inebriate—yon ethereal blue!

O princely state, to walk with nature free,
Untrammelled by the stuccoed forms of town—
Diamonds in every flower, an arch in every tree,
And the Court dress, an unpretending gown;

Sing on excursive Locusts, for the gloom
From yonder City, soon must be your tomb!

Its reeking odors, and its hollow hearts;
The forms of London and of Paris aped;
Where gilded splendor from the sewer starts,
Society as well as sewer shaped
By the same hand, with superscription drear,
"Nature abandon, ye who enter here!"*

Now grateful shades, to mossy banks invite,
Cool waters murmuring as they wander slow
Where silvery fishes leaping to the light,
Or nibbling at the hook, that sinks below,
Give promise of a simple feast at night,
Where sweet contentment sheds eternal light!

Watching the cork that dances down below,
I wander back to infancy in vain,
Its very pin-hooks, dangle to and fro,
And tiny hands are clasping them again—
Sweet buriéd hands; one kiss before we part—
O, let me press you to my bleeding heart!

Thus dreaming oft, I gaze on many a face,
Dearer than life—now lost forevermore!
Then look to Heaven, but failing there to trace
Their flying feet, survey the silent shore—
No foot-print there, no laughter on the wind—
The landscape fades, as tears of sorrow blind.

---

*——Lassat oigni speranza.

Barney now drives his lowing herd afield
And faithful Bridget follows, with her eyes
Measuring what milk the foaming buckets yield;
Of Barney dreams, and blesses with her sighs.
Ye roses, honeysuckles, hay new mown,
Those honeyéd sighs are sweeter than your own!

Barney will come again at eventide,
But ere that hour, she listens for the cows;
Surveys the pasture and the mountain side,
Only to see what way the cattle browse,
But all unconscious what a gathering storm,
What hopes and fears, her gentle bosom warm.

Behold yon reapers in the noon-day sun,
Hark to their songs, advancing to the strife;
Where the proud swain had many a victory won—
Pride of the village, and his plume in life;
Now marshalled all, they stand in bright array,
Cradle in hand, and ready for the fray.

And now the lofty Rye, like Cossacks tall,
Shoulder to shoulder, each with plumed head,
Defies the Cycle, lo, battalions fall!
But from the ground a brighter lustre shed,
Like soldiers, when to cycled death they yield,
Still bright, with glory, on the Battlefield!

'Tis harvest home—yon maiden claps her hands,
Her Barney leads the Battle, with its din—
And now the reapers sit about in bands
All wondering how the slender youth could win—

'Twas nature's self—yon maid with pretty zone,
Inspired his scythe, and made it all her own.

Now, hand in hand, they wander to the spring,
Yon willow branches veil the bride and groom;
O, trespass not thou base luxurious thing,
From lofty couch, in yonder gilded room—
Nature's pure offering—that mossy seat,
Where Heaven and earth in sweet communion meet.*

Yon sexéd flowers, tho' placed by Heaven apart,
Are joined by insects, bearing to and fro,
Sweet Pollen, passionate as human heart,
Wherever forests wave, and flowers blow;
For this, on humming bird, the roses smile,
And honeyed drops Hymeneal bees beguile.†

For this yon wild pink sends up to the sky,
Its spicy odors—spreads its colors sweet—
Hoping to lure the wanton butterfly,
From other flowers, with gold upon his feet;
Conscious as man (but in a low degree)
A living soul, without its spirit free.

Not this the love yon painted creature knows,
Sending a ghastly smile from teeth of ice,

---

*Minnehaha Springs, Parthenon Grove.
†Darwin has demonstrated that flowers have a seeming consciousness, and lure by their beauty, as well as their sweetness, the various insects, which convey the pollen to their bosoms. Even St. Thomas Aquinas distinguishes between the sensual and spiritual soul, and the sphinx moth leaves his dove-like image on the flower, "*Le St. Esprit.*" The *Catholic Review* says "that orchids are fertilized by bees, moths, butterflies and various insects. A very strange property belongs to many of them. Their bloom takes on a weird, inexplicable resemblance to the insect which carries the pollen from one flower to another."

Observed of all observers, how she goes
With wimpling step—her corset for a vice—
Nor love like his—yon dude's in fashion's style;
Simpering to win her mercenary smile.

Rather the love of yonder children fair,
Two baby lovers—catching butterflies—
Quoth she, "what kind of birds are these, my dear?"
Quoth he, "What kind o' birds? Ha! Ha!" His eyes
Upon his baby sweet, his heart and cheek aglow,
With happiness that art can never know.

For this the lip of Beauty with its dews—
Thine own, O Nature, every look and tone!
Inspired by thee—the trembling lover sues,
'Til wrapped Elysium clasps her yielding zone;
Yet fools there be where yonder sages plod,
Dissevering all this happiness from God!

Now thunder clouds come marching up the sky,
With lighter couriers, dashing to and fro;
What fearful beauties break upon the eye;
What awful thunders shake the world below,
What lightnings flash, what stormy wind and rain,
What floods, O Nature, desolate the plain!

Now clouds conceal thee, veiled the more in showers,
New charms unfolding, in thy matchless form;
So passing beautiful, in sunny bowers—
More lovely now, tho' dreadful as the storm;
And yonder rainbow, climbing up the skies,
Like hope illusive, lights them up and dies—

Illusive? Aye—yon maiden at the spring,
Poor Barney's head upon her pulseless breast,
Both smitten by the lightning's fiery wing;
Their hopes and fears forevermore at rest!
O, better thus, than wrinkled o'er with care
To sink into the grave without a loving tear.

Better, ten thousand times, than watch a flower,
Budding and blooming up to manhood's form;
To find upon it, in a mournful hour,
Debauchery, more dreadful than the storm—
Keener than lightnings, to dissolve the soul,
And hurl it down where louder thunders roll!

O, better thus, like yonder rainbow spring
To beaming happiness, on Beauty's smile,
Then fly from tempest, on the lightning's wing,
Than plod along, thro' many a weary mile,
Only to find the Paradise we claim,
Planted with thorns, and covered o'er with shame.

In long array, now winding from the grove,
Yon burial escort bears its dead along;
The birds are silent, save that yonder dove
Gives back antiphonal the funeral song.
If this be all, O, Sexton, hold awhile!
Let Hope expire, and Nature cease to smile!

But see yon rainbow! Sexton, let them down,
No Princely chamber has a stronger wall;

No Monarch claims a more enduring crown;
For who can covet what must come to all?
Its ice-cold band, as cold on Bridget now,
As when it fell on Cleopatra's brow!

Gone is the rainbow, with its laughing rain;
Symbolical of human hopes and fears;
Earth's sweetest joy, the counterpart of pain,
As the bright rainbow, redolent of tears;
Sing on ye songsters—bloom ye flowers bright,
For Nature's next vicissitude is night.

Toss, toss, your diamonds O, ecstatic grove,
Throw your sweet kisses to returning peace;
The Heavens bow down, to bless you with their love;
The clouds are passing, and the showers cease;
In bridal beauty kiss the wanton wind,
With a sweet love that leaves no sting behind!

Farewell to Bridget—Barney faretheewell!
The great may smile, contemptuous of my lyre,
That finds a moment with your dust to dwell,
While tears unbidden quench its wonted fire.
Your virtues plead, and angels bend to hear
What splendor scorns and wicked spirits fear.

Splendor indeed! (?)   See Hildebrand afar!
When shall mankind behold another man?
Prince of all Princes—Earth's sublimest star,
His *peasant* mother in the Vatican!

Jesus and Joseph—Mary ye despise—
Look up, and see the splendor of the skies!

Who now lifts up his trumpet voice in Rome,
Defending labor?—holding to his heart
His children as a mother in her home,
From whom her bosom cannot, will not part!
Say who, while Gibbons struggles for the poor,
Despise their tears, and drive them from the door!

Who rule the Nations?—not yon groveling lords—
Filthy Lord Campbell, nor the filthier Duke,
Luring a wanton by lascivious words,
Till the heart sickens and the nations p—ke!
O, what are they to yonder Prince refined,
His only heritage a heavenly mind!

Say, who the princes living on like stars,
Bound to no pent-up continent or shore—
Above the world—above Ambition's wars,
Living and shining on forevermore!
From Hildebrand to Gibbons, see your kings;
And learn to smile upon yon meaner things.

Yes, smile upon them, but with merry laugh,
Behold their silly apes in Washington;
O, turn my lyre from such unworthy chaff,
And gaze upon your Dead at Parthenon.

To Bridget turn, whose dust is sleeping here,
And pay to innocence a parting tear.*

---

*Pope Gregory VII gave directions that his mother should be presented to his court in her own peasant dress—a coarse gown and wooden shoes:

> Yet "Flora McFlimsey had nothing to wear!"
> And Harris, though drunk as a goat,
> Like Garland, the modest, would never appear
> Exposed in a swallow-tail coat.

How could the Senator find it in his heart to call the Author's poetry "*doggerels*," while giving testimony *on oath*, before "The Congressional Committee?" Do not his letters, now before me, praise the author, and his poems to the skies? but, alas! this poor man was then lapping milk from the "*Pan*," which may still be seen on his beard, whenever he enters the Senate! Apollo, for a like offence, when Midas preferred *Pan music* to his *divine songs*, changed him to an Ass!

> *Pana* jubet Tmolus citharæ submittere cannas.
> Judicium sanctique placet sententia montis
> Omnibus: arguitur tamen, atque injusta vocatur
> Unius sermone Midæ. Nec Delius aures
> Humanam stolidas patitur retinere figuram,
> Sed trahit in spatium, villisque albentibus implet,
> Instabilesque illas facit, et dat posse moveri,
> Cætera sunt hominis; partem damnatur in unam,
> Induiturque aures lente gradientis aselli.

But, perhaps, Midas was only after *milk* when he praised old Pan—God of the *flocks*, for Ovid adds:

> Isque, deum *pecoris* spectans: Dixit!

END OF "SPRING."

Summer, Autumn, and Winter are now ready for publication, but await the judgment of the Public on the First Part.

APPENDIX

(A B)

Original Contract and Synopsis of Bill

BY

JAMES CHARLES ROGERS, Esq.

IN THE

Supreme Court of the District of Columbia.

GENERAL TERM, JAN. 1887.

IN EQUITY.

J. HARRIS ROGERS,
vs.
U. S. Att'y Gen'l AUGUSTUS H. GARLAND,
Senator ISHAM G. HARRIS,
Member Congress CASEY YOUNG,
Indian Com'r J. D. C. ATKINS,
R. R. Com'r JOSEPH E. JOHNSTON,
} DOCKET 10,051

Hon. JOHN CRITCHER,
J. W. ROGERS,
JOHN CRITCHER, Jr.,
JAMES CHARLES ROGERS,
} COUNSELLORS FOR PLAINTIFF.

PROPOSITION TO DEFENDANTS, UNDER WHICH, BY ACCEPTING, THEY ACQUIRED THEIR RESPECTIVE INTERESTS IN COMPLAINANT'S VARIOUS PROPERTIES.

[Exhibits "A" and "C" of the bill.]

We, therefore, propose to public consideration a powerful corporation to possess, a little in the future, vast laboratories, learned electricians, and skilled mechanics, standing ready to seize upon and develope whatever may be presented in the light of its influence, capital and genius—nor, would it seem extravagant to say that such a corporation, with its new methods, might convert great coal fields into torrents of electricity—that it might, in time, harness the very waves, clouds, water-falls and winds to generate this mysterious agent of nature—and that busy marts and thoroughfares, with their bankers, tradesmen and pompous fashions, may soon be seen thousands of miles distant through the *telemorphe*, riding in carriages without horses, cars without steam—all lighted up by electric suns, in a new and enchanting civilization!

One-tenth interest will be sold, only to monied men applying for it, at a merely nominal price, to construct machinery, and other interests will be sold at auction on the New York Stock Exchange for what it may bring; but it is confidently predicted that the stock will ultimately go greatly above par. It may require years to affect this result, for we depend in no way upon Stock jobbing operations, but upon a manly and scientific developement of real values which stand on their intrinsic merits.

Parties investing, must examine through their own electricians, experts and lawyers, who will judge whether the inventions are valuable or not; so that if they should, by unseen possibilities be less valuable than we suppose, no stockholders can plead ignorance. It is a venture for enormous profits or a trifle—the Company has so ventured, and would rather keep its stock and take its own chance of profit and loss, than to be responsible for the many defects which exist in every new invention.

CONTRACT OF THE PAN-ELECTRIC STATESMEN, BY WHICH THEY GAVE THE VERBAL CONTRACT A WRITTEN FORM.

[Exhibit " B."]

"Be it known that these articles of agreement, drawn up and entered into in the city and State of New York, on the 13th of March, eighteen hundred and eighty-three, by and between James Harris Rogers, a resident of the city of Washington, in the District of Columbia; of Joseph E. Johnston, also a resident of the city of Washington, in the District of Columbia; Augustus H. Garland, a resident of the city of Little Rock, in the State of Arkansas; John D. C. Atkins, a resident of the city of Paris, in the county of Henry, in the State of Tennessee; Isham G. Harris, and Casey Young, residents of the city of Memphis, in the State of Tennessee, witnesseth:

"That, whereas the said James Harris Rogers is the owner of sundry valuable improvements, discoveries, and inventions in respect to and concerning the various uses, properties, and application of electricity, as a heating, lighting, motive, transmitting, and receiving power of agency, and which said improvements, discoveries and inventions are secured to aforesaid James Harris Rogers, by Letters Patent, already issued to him as the author thereof, or by application filed therefor, in the office of the Commissioner of Patents of the United States of

America, the same being known, designated and described as follows: that is, those which are already patented, to wit:

"'An Invention, styled Embossed Telegraph,' and numbered on the books of the Patent Office in Washington City, No. 130,662.

"'An Invention for improvement of Electric Light,' numbered 216,760.

"'An Invention for a Central Telephonic System,' numbered 268,294.

"'An Invention for a Telephonic Repeater,' numbered 269,326.

"Upon all of which patents have been already granted to the aforesaid James Harris Rogers. There is also embraced in these articles of agreement the following inventions, for which applications for patents have been made to wit:

"'An Invention for Cylindrical Automatic Telegraphy,' numbered 87,340.

"'An Invention styled a Telephonic] Transmitter,' numbered 80,5 5.

"'An Inventioned styled the Duplex and Quadruplex Telegraph,' numbered 15,734.

"'An Invention styled Thermotelemetre,' numbered 16,933.

"An Invention styled a Sub-marine Cable with insulation, numbered 69,966, only one-half of which last mentioned invention is, however, included in these articles of agreement. For all of the last-mentioned inventions, applications have been filed in the Patent Office as aforesaid. And there is also embraced in this agreement the following inventions, for which no patents have been issued, nor applications made for the same; but which the said James Harris Rogers proposes hereafter to obtain, if the same can be obtained from the Commissioner of Patents, to wit: 'Igniting Gas by Dynamo Machines;' 'Generating Electricity directly from Coal;' 'An Electrical Enumerator and Calculator,' and all other inventions and discoveries in electricity heretofore made by the said James Harris Rogers, the title to which still remains in him.

"And whereas the said James Harris Rogers is desirous of further developing and putting into practical working operation the improvements, discoveries, and inventions, and for the purpose of obtaining the aid and assistance in the furtherance and accomplishment of this object of the persons herein named, is also desirous of forming an association or joint stock company with the said Joseph E. Johnston, Augustus H. Garland, John D. C. Atkins, Isham G. Harris, and Casey Young.

"Now, therefore, all the above-named persons hereby mutually agree to constitute themselves an association or joint stock company, for the objects and purposes above set out, upon the following terms and stipulations:

"First. It is mutually agreed and understood by all the parties hereto, that as among themselves, the value of said improvements, discoveries, and inventions, shall be estimated at one million dollars.

"That this amount shall be divided in ten (10) equal parts or shares, four of which are to be held and owned by the said James Harris Rogers, and one (1) each by the said Jos. E. Johnston, Augustus H. Garland, John D. C. Atkins, Isham G. Harris, and Casey Young; and the other part or shares shall be jointly held by the company to be disposed of in such a manner as the members thereof think fit.

"Second. It is further mutually agreed by the parties to this agreement, that they will, as soon as the same can be done, procure a charter of incorporation, constituting themselves a corporate body, under the name and style of the 'Pan-Electric Company" embracing under such charter of incorporation such objects and powers as they may deem proper and as are allowed to incorporate bodies under the laws of the State of New York, or of any other State in which said charter of incorporation may be obtained.

"Third. It is also agreed that when the aforesaid persons are incorporated as a corporate body, as hereinbefore provided, all the capital stock of said corporation shall be the joint property of this company, and it may issue, sell, or otherwise dispose of so much thereof as they may see fit, provided that no individual member shall dispose of any interest acquired under these articles of agreement at less than the face value thereof without the assent of the executive committee, hereinafter provided for.

"And all interests, jointly held by the company, and which may be sold as aforesaid, and disposed of by direction of the aforesaid executive committee, shall be sold for the joint benefit of the company.

Provided further, That the said James Harris Rogers shall have the right to dispose of, to such persons as he may see fit, an interest in the property of the company hereinbefore enumerated, amounting to the sum of one hundred and seventy thousand dollars ($170,000) upon the basis of a capital stock of five millions of dollars ($5,000,000).

"Fourth. It is also further stipulated and agreed that the aforesaid parties to this agreement may admit others to membership in this Association or company upon such terms and conditions as they may prescribe; it being understood that they are the joint owners of all the properties, rights of franchises herein set out or referred to.

"Fifth. And it is also agreed that until the said charter of incorporation shall be procured, the company organized, and the board of directors elected thereunder, there shall be chosen from the persons above mentioned an executive committee of three who shall conduct the business and affairs of the company, and direct the doing of such things as may be needed to do for the furtherance of the objects herein set out. And any expenses incurred for the doing of the same, may assess pro rata upon the members of the company to the amount of one hundred and fifty dollars ($150) each; and no greater sum shall be assessed without authority from a majority of the members.

"And should any member be unwilling to pay the amount which may be assessed against him as aforesaid, he may withdraw from the company upon such terms as the remaining members thereof may impose or he may be expelled by a majority vote; the persons so withdrawing, or being expelled, shall, however, be acquitted of all liability to the company or on its account.

"Sixth. The parties to this instrument hereby stipulated and agree to pay in the manner, and to the amount hereinbefore specified, the expense which may be necessarily incurred in perfecting the inventions, discoveries, and improvements herein set out and in practically demonstrating their uses and value.

"Seventh. And in consideration of the last preceding article, it is stipulated and agreed by the said James Harris Rogers that any improvements which he may hereafter make upon any of the discoveries or inventions embraced in this instrument, or any further inventions or discoveries which he may make that are necessary to perfect those already made, applied for, or in contemplation, shall be the joint property of the Pan-Electric Company, provided, however, that the company shall pay any expense he may incur in making the same.

"Eighth. The executive committee hereinbefore provided for, shall have the power, if in their judgment the same shall become necessary for the furtherance of the objects and purposes of this Association to agree with other parties to sell them such interests in the properties of this company or association as they may see proper, giving such persons a written or printed certificate, in which it shall be stipulated that the purchasers of such interest shall receive therefor a certificate for such share or shares of stock in the Pan Electric Company, when organized, at such a valuation as the said executive committee may determine upon.

"And it is agreed that said executive committee shall consist of Joseph E. Johnston, James Harris Rogers, and Casey Young.

"Ninth. The domicile or place of business of this company or association shall for the present be in the city of Washington, District of Columbia.

"Tenth. These articles of agreement may be altered or amended at any time at the option of two-thirds of the parties in interest.

"In witness of all of which we have hereunto set our seals, in the city and state aforesaid, on the day and date above written.

"JAMES HARRIS ROGERS, [SEAL.]
JOSEPH E. JOHNSTON. [SEAL.]
By his attorney-in fact, ISHAM G. HARRIS.
A. H. GARLAND. [SEAL.]
By his attorney-in-fact. ISHAM G. HARRIS.
JOHN D. C. ATKINS. [SEAL]
ISHAM G. HARRIS. [SEAL.]
CASEY YOUNG." [SEAL.]

SYNOPSIS OF COMPLAINANT'S BILL.

I.

(1). Defendants got possession of complainants property without ever paying any one of the MANY considerations promised.

Sections 5, 6, 8, 9, 39, 40.

( ). Defendants were guilty of committing *Gross frauds* upon complainant, which though not set out *in totidem verbis*, are apparent in the facts admitted by the demurrer. (Sections 15, 30, 37, 38, 39, 40). (Demurrer should have denied fraud and conspiracy).

II.

(1). Whether "the association" was a partnership or not, it was certainly a *joint stock* company, *in embrio*, which printed the stock promised, but refused to issue the same, or give the complainant the part of it for which he had *paid*. (Sections 9, 15, 16). Preamble to Exhibit B, immediately before Section First.

III.

Whatever "the association" may have been, the defendants broke faith with, and defrauded the complainant as follows:

(1). If no joint stock company was formed, by *not forming it*. (Sections 5, 9, Exhibit B).

(2). If no partnership was formed, by not forming it, (same).

(3). By not *attempting* to procure the universal charter, which they promised to assist in procuring, and by not issuing its stock or any stock when they became apprehensive that *stock jobbing* would interfere with their political aspirations. (Sections 5, 6, 9, 10, 20, 25, 27, 30, 31, 39, 40).

(4). By refusing to *issue*, even to the present time the *joint stock company stock* and the Telegraph company stock, after prevailing on plaintiff to assign his patents and after putting him to the expense of printing both these stocks. (Sections 36, also 43, 41, 44, 49, unprinted).

(5.) By refusing to issue the telephone stock, (the only patents in litigation) until too late to use it on account of *litigation*. (Same.)

(6.) By drawing large amounts of money without complainant's consent, from mere *bald* sales of his patents; which sales they never, themselves, even effected, but complainant's agent, Loony, did. (29, 39.)

(7.) By appropriating large sums, by his consent, which

they fraudulently obtained, by false promises, and in this instance more money than he ever consented to. (29, 39.)

(8.) By keeping from him the books of all the companies, so that he could never get an account from either. (Sections 50 and 51.)

(9.) By "jumbling all the accounts together in a disorderly manner, and holding complainants moneys thereunder, without ever rendering him an account conformable to his rights. (Sections 29, 50, 51.)

(10.) By inducing plaintiff, by false promises, to sell interests for money in which they participated to his disadvantage. (29, 34.)

(11.) By retaining interests in his patents *yet unsold*, and holding the same tied up *against "public policy"* to the *restraint of trade*. (39.)

(12.) By retaining moneys for which *part interests* were sold for the *un-*incorporated company, such as Senator Vest's. (24, 29 and Ex. G.)

(13.) By retaining the stocks for which other interests were sold to corporations. (24, 34.)

(14.) By retaining money from State rights, sold by the Telephone Company, controlled by themselves (see 35) without giving complainant either all his stock in said Telephone Company (which Casey Young swears before the Congressional Committee to be due complainant, but withheld by his—Young's—"*mistake*,") or a just proportion of money and local stocks as dividends due him, (Sec's 24, 29, 34.)

(15.) By so confusing the numerous company accounts, that many suits at law would become necessary to approximate their settlement. (Sections 50, 51, 24, 29, 34.)

(16.) By holding plaintiff's property so bound, that they can, at any time procure the universal charter promised, which, if *against public policy*, he, *non pari delicto*, now wishes to *prevent*. (Prayers for dissolution—especially prayer for general relief.)

Hence complainant says that their demurrer admits all

these things to be true, and that they should not be permitted to come in at the eleventh hour *whining that their contract was against public policy;* and that therefore they may go off with complainant's money and patents.
He therefore prays:
First. (If a partnership exists) that it may be dissolved and accounts taken, &c.
Second. If it does not exist, that under the *general prayer, part owners* be dealt with in Equity according to universal practice. (Adam's Equity 247.)
Third. That a recision be made *quoad* what the defendants, as *individuals,* now hold or claim in the premises; and that they be required to turn to the plaintiff all his unsold inventions now tied up, *against public policy,* and running to *waste*—4 years in the life of patents, admitted by defendants, to be worth millions to the public. (Exhibit A and C.)
Fourth. That they be required to transfer to plaintiff all the stocks and moneys which they have *unjustly acquired, directly, or indirectly, from his inventions;* and such other things as the Honorable Court may decree.

[Appendix C, page 27.]

It is certainly worthy of observation that *Rome* was acknowledged by the whole world to be the centre and seat of Christianity—the very *rock* on which her " anchor was thrown !"

Is it not marvellous that all the Fathers (nearly all in conquered provinces where Rome was hated) should without hesitation acknowledge this overbearing and tyranical city, instead of Jerusalem or Antioch (even while the tyrant was persecuting), to be the head or centre of Christianity ? All the holy fathers lifted their hands and hearts with awe and veneration to Rome.

Hermas, spoken of by St. Paul, in his epistle to the

Romans, chapter XVI, sends his theological book "*Pastor*" to the *Roman Inquisition* if you please, to be examined and approved by Pope Clement, who is also spoken of in Scripture—not to the Bishop of Jerusalem nor Antioch nor yet to St. John, then living, but to *Rome!*

St. Ignatius, instructed by an apostle—the breath of St. John still warm on his head, proclaims the decisions of the Pope authoritative for the whole world:

Quae docendo praecipitis.

St. Polycarp, old and decrepid (nearly 80 years of age) destined soon to embrace the flames, makes a painful journey from France to Rome, to consult Pope St. Anicetus, on the subject of Easter—Why, Jeff Davis would hardly visit Cleveland by rail to ask his guidance—being himself President of a Republic; but thousands of statesmen do. Is it because Cleveland lives in a big town? O, no, it is because he has *Jurisdiction* over the whole country.

St. Irenaeus, St. Polycarp's disciple, exclaims: "All the Churches necessarily hang on Rome, as the waters depend on the *fountain*, and as the body depends on its *head*" (excuse this too literal, and yet too prolix translation; I am not aiming at elegant diction but *truth*). His very words are: Omnes a Roma Eclesia necesse est pendent, tanquam a fonte et capite.* Again: *ad hanc enim Eclesiam necesse est omnem connenire Eclesiam, in qua ab his, qui sunt undique fideles conservata est ea, quae ab apostolis est, traditio.*

For it is *necessary* for all the churches to *come together*, at this Church, in which is preserved, *through the faithful everywhere, that tradition which is from the Apostles*—Indeed! Did the faithful, from every quarter of the globe, bend their steps to Rome, and there

---

*Iven. Lib. 3. Ado. Heres: 4 l. 5. Adv. Heres.

deposit all the traditions, even before the great *tradition* the *New Testament*, had been authoritatively collected, and promulgated by the Pope! Again (translated by Father Weneger) he says; "If we remain firm in our allegiance to the *See of St. Peter*, we shall easily disconcert the malice of those who, either through conceitedness or bad faith, broach new fangled themes at variance with sound doctrine."

Tertullian, also of the 2d century, says: "I learn that an *edict* has been promulgated, and that indeed the Sovereign Pontiff—Bishop of Bishops—has proclaimed it peremptory!" Peremptory? Cæsar? Cleveland? No—the Pope!

Tertullian, who seems to have fallen entirely from the Catholic faith and become a Montanist (the Millerites of antiquity), was, nevertheless, the most learned of men, and, therefore, a competent witness to the *fact*, that when the apostles were scarcely cold in their graves, and when Calvary was yet radiant, and warm, and dear to the hearts of Christians, a city far away from their dear Jerusalem, and envied and hated by the Provinces, was, nevertheless, acknowledged to be the *See of Peter*, the *centre of Christianity*, and the *source of all ecclesiastical jurisdiction*. But why pursue the subject of patristic testimony? Origen, St. Cyprian, St. Jerome, St. Basil, St. Augustin Ongin, all—all are unanimous, exclaiming:

Roma locuta, causa finita est: Quod non *armis, Religioni* vicisti, urbs Aeterna!*

---

* Jam, modo, qua fuerant silvæ pecorumque recessus,
　Urbs erat, æternæ quum pater *urbis* ait:
　Arbiter armorum, de cujus, sanguine natus
　Credor; et, ut credar pignora multa dabo:
　A te principium romano ducimus anno ;
　　Primus de patrio nomine mensis eat.))
　Vox rata fit; patrioque vocat de nomine mensem.
　　Dicitur hæc pietas grata fuisse deo.

[Page 30, Appendix "D."]

What stupendous folly to suppose that civilization and learning came with the 16th century! And yet, how many learned knaves beguile the multitude by asserting it!

Already had Bernado chanted his *Amadige*, and all Christendom, though disturbed for a term by Luther, still hangs with delight on Tasso's harp. Dante, nearly 300 years before the great rebellion in Germany and England, had traversed Heaven and earth and hell. The lurid flames of his *Inferno* still startle each rising generation, and furnish great sermons for preachers. Boccacio, surpassing Orpheus, sang his *Teseide*; invented *Ottava rima*, and stayed the black plague by arresting fear and dread as he beguiled the imagination with his immortal Decamerone.

PAINTING.

Titian, Raphael, and Michael Angelo had brought all Heaven down on canvas, while their predecessors and disciples filled Europe with monuments of art that still survive, and must live forever.

Titian was born 30 years before the Reformation; attracted universal admiration, and was invited to the courts of Pope Leo the 10th and Charles V. Though born 30 years before the Reformation, he was not by any means the founder of his art in Italy; for, as a modern Protestant beautifully expresses it, "he broke completely away from the intensity of *Florentine art* and the mysticism of the *Sienese*, and turned to revel in the material grandeur which had *reached its height in the pride of Venetian luxury.* His style is large and sane, like his nature, and his art a golden mean of joy, unbroken by a brusque movement of the passions!"

"His was the vigor of exquisitely balanced faculties; his, above all, the sublime sense of color and the mastery of pure tints in subtle interplay. Each master-piece is a chromatic symphony, aglow with the fervor of Venetian sunset, luminous with the haze of lagoons, shot through with the inmost purple of light, radiant with the pearly gleam of flesh, tremulous with silver light and golden mysteries of shadow." "There is," says Ruskin, "a strange undercurrent of everlasting murmur about his name, which means the deep consent of all great men that he is greater than they; that there is a softness more exquisite than Corrigio's; a purity loftier than Leonardo's; a force mightier than Rembrandt's; a serenity more awful than Raphael's!

But why pursue the subject of painting to see whether civilization came with poor Martin Luther?

SCULPTURE.

Who but Phydias, and his disciples in Greece, ever made "the marble speak," until Catholicity developed sculpture in Europe? Even the Romans of antiquity produced no great sculptor.

Pizarro's "*deposition from the Cross*" appeared, and preached its great sermons to mankind just 300 years before Henry VIII beheld the lovely form of Annie Boleyn, and more than 250 years before Martin Luther had kissed his apostate nun. Even before the time of Pizarro, Catholic artists had covered the facades of Lombardy with dramatic groups of surpassing loveliness, and gothic artists adorned the churches and porches of Europe with unrivalled forms of beauty. In the 15th century Catholic Germany gave to religion and art the great works of Vischer, Schönhoffer, and Kraff. The Tuscan masters— Dela Quercia, Brumelleschi, Ghiberti, and Donatello, enchanted mankind and developed civilization. The Gates of the Florentine Abbey, by Ghiberti, are supreme specimens of art, and the names of Robia, Gucci, Benedito, bring us to the Renaissance, lighted up by the genius of Michael Angelo. "He moulded," says a Protestant writer, "the mixed motives of contemporary sculpture into marvelous ideals of vehement motion and Dantesque dignity." Dante, Titian, Michael Angelo! Their very names a watchtower and a light forever! And yet, we are gravely told by preachers, that all these thousand luminaries, already referred to, were as nothing compared to Henry VIII, Luther, Calvin, Servetus, and Annie Boleyn? That the court of Pope Leo X, beaming with science, letters, art, and piety; pales before the painted courtiers of Elizabeth, and that the whole world was a chaos, until passion gratified, rose up and invented lucifer matches, Plymouth Church, the Salvation Army, and dynamite!

MUSIC.

Divine music had already enchanted the world, and the spirit of St. Cecilia lifted mankind to the gate of Heaven. A monk had invented the gamut 500 years before the lascivious songs of the 16th century began to attract mankind. "A Climbing up the Golden Stairs" was then unknown, and its author, now in the penitentiary, had not been born. The church, however, had adopted all that was grand and awful and sublime in music, while the most gentle and refined society sighed to the harp, or danced to the rebec, for there was nothing sombre about Catholic civilization; and yet, an exquisite and beautiful, but dim, religious light pervaded everything. If Raphael and Michael Angelo knelt to the Blessed Virgin when they took their pencils, so in every art religion was honored; and musical notation, just referred to, as invented by a Benedictine monk in Arizzo, was sanctified by the hymn to St. John 500 years before Henry VIII in *an ex post facto* acrostic:

    Ut queant laxis
    Resonare fibris,
    Mira gestorum
    Famuli tuorum;
    Solve polluti
    Labii reatum,
    Sancte Ioannes.*

* Ut, re, mi, fa, so, la, sa.

In the 14th and 15th centuries great advances developed this art. Joaquin des Pres was known all over Europe. Pare's *Italian opera, Eurydice,* was sung in Florence before the 16th century, and but for these developments of a purely Catholic art, neither Handel, Haydn, Mozart, Beethoven, Cherubini, Rossini, nor Bach might now be known.

[Appendix "O," page 39.]

In Prince George's County, five miles northeast of Washington, is Green Hill, the manor house of Chillam Castle Manor, portion of an old grant of 8,000 acres to Dudley Diggs, of the family of Sir Dudley Digges of Chillam Castle, England, (Chiselholme,) Master of the Rolls under King Charles I.

In a copse of cedars, in a secluded spot, in the garden, not far from the mansion, is the ancient family burial place. The ruins of the tenements of the former denizens of the hallowed soil lie crumbling around. Three lonely and unmarked graves remain to commemorate the solemn former uses of the spot. In the largest, over six feet in length, lies what remains after 61 years of the perishable mortality of Major Peter Charles L'Enfant. His only companions in that garden of death are a child and a suicide, buried by superstitious slaves diagonally in his grave. The fond hands of kindred and friends have tenderly conveyed to consecrated ground the remains of those who once gathered here, as the skeleton harvester made his rounds. A sighing pine, drawing its vigorous life from the very earth which envelopes the ashes of L'Enfant, attuned by the breezes of heaven, carries the inspiration of his genius into never-ending requiem. Nature, more generous than man, has drawn over the lonely mound a mantle of myrtle, like a pall of perennial green.

L'ENFANT'S CAREER.

The career of L'Enfant and its sequel presents a touching illustration of the munificent gifts of genius, the nobility of a human soul, the littleness of men, and the ingratitude of a nation. Peter Charles L'Enfant was born in France about 1755. He was an officer in the French line. He came to America about 1777, and gave his heart and sword to the cause of liberty. In 1778 he was a captain of engineers in the continental army. His bravery was displayed on every occasion. At Savannah he was badly wounded and taken prisoner in the assault by Count D'Estang. In 1782 he was exchanged, and a year later was promoted to major of engineers.

THE PLAN OF WASHINGTON.

This priceless souvenir of the nation's capital in embryo, much faded by the lapse of time, is preserved in the office of Col. John M. Wilson, engineer in charge of public buildings and grounds. Washington meddled with it somewhat in the interests of a speculating friend who owned land, and marred the symmetry and beauty of the grounds in the front of the President's house. The execution of the plan commenced by its projector did not long remain in his hands. One of the discreditable acts of Washington was his treatment of the accomplished engineer. The powerful Carroll, of Duddington, having built a house in one of the avenues laid down on the plan, the engineer proceeded to remove it. Washington, in 1792, yielded to the injustice of Carroll's demands, and, against the wishes of many interested in the carrying forward of the work, assented to L'Enfant's removal.—*Washington paper.*

Pan-electric statesmen may now plume themselves on finding a *glorious precedent!* But the Supreme Court, now trying the Pan-Electric case, however grateful for Mr. Cleveland's and Garland's *patronage*, will not repay their *favors* by crying out "*Ecrassez L'Enfant!*"

[Appendix " MN," page 48.]

The fallen oak thus complained to an unknown tree, supposed to be the large hickory still standing by the spring, where the author and Col. Looney sported in prosperity.

> Conquerar, an taceam ? ponam sine nomine crimen ?
> An notum, qui sis, omnibus esse velim ?
> Nomine non utar, ne commendere querela,
> Quæraturque tibi carmine fama meo.
> Dum mea puppis erat valida fundata carina,
> Qui mecum velles currere primus eras.
> Nunc, quia contrixit vultum Fortuna, recedis,
> Auxilio postquam scis opus esse tuo.

ARCHITECTURE.

An architecture, purely Catholic, filled the Christian world ; and its ruins, smouldering from the so-called Reformation, still sigh for the civilization on which its turrets looked when they rose a thousand years ago.

Abbeys, like Westminster, and cathedrals, like that of Cologne, (founded or improved by Charlemaigne and Edward the Confessor, whose arches continue to soar, like the expanding wings of angels, to the groined roof, are still gazed upon by modern preachers with breathless awe ; amazed, perhaps, that Art had honored God in " *the dark ages* !"

What wonder that the Catholic church should develop a new and sublime architecture ? Was it not hers to break down the temples of paganism, and yet to gather the world, which she was commissioned to teach, in suitable places, symbolical of Heaven ? Is she not the mother of European civilization, and have not her children written nearly all the books in the world ? Cobden one of England's greatest Protestant statesmen, being himself astonished, astonished still more his countrymen, by his proffer to find in any biographical dictionary of great men, three Catholic names for every Protestant celebrity, and thoughtful men know that the latter, so few in number, derive all their noble and lofty inspirations from Catholic sources. Even Voltaire, *protesting* against every-

thing holy, rises above himself (says Chateaubriand) only when his dramatic characters require a Christian mould.

OTHER ARTS.

Long before Germany had gazed upon her prodigious infant kicking in his cradle at Eisleiben; the mariner's compass had been introduced into Europe; Roger Bacon had developed electricity, and made a "talking man"—perhaps the telephone—but no Pan-Electric statesmen were found in the House of (Catholic) Lords to cheat poor Roger at Oxford. Arabian figures had also been introduced by the Crusades. The art of navigation by sails had been developed, and even steam navigation, (when the wars of Protestant princes retarded civilization,) just emerging from experiment to practice, became a "*lost art.*" A steamer crossed the bay of Barcelona in the presence of Charles V and his court, but the Reformation retarded everything except passion, and very little more was done with steam until James Watt invented his engine, but Catholic France had opened the way for Fulton, who studied under Livingtone's patronage in St. Genevieve, and doubless received from Catholic sources what had there been invented, but long forgotten. The University of Paris, which instructed Fulton, had been established by Charlemaigne over 500 years before Luther was born. Pisa, Boulougna and Magdeburg had filled Europe with learning long before the art of printing sprang from the bosom of the Catholic church. She immediately applied this art to instruct and convert mankind. Aldus Manutius printed the first Polyglot; and Cardinal Ximines, at his own cost of 50,000 ducats, published at Alcada his Complutesian Polyglot in many languages. Even benighted Africans had read the genuine Scriptures in their own vernacular long before Henry VIII rejected as spurious those books of the Bible which most inculcated offerings for the dead, whose treasures he wished to lavish on his lust. The great Cardinal, to accomplish the good work of giving many Bibles to mankind, drew to his university the most learned men of Europe, practiced almost incredible austerities, and died a saint in the very year that Luther married the apostate nun, and when Anne Boleyn was yet an infant.

Prescott, our own Protestant historian, in his "Ferdinand and Isabella," seems to think that such a thing as piety was known before it had been monopolized by modern passion, and pays a glowing tribute to this great publisher of Bibles. "He died," says Prescott, "at Toledo, November 8, 1517. He lived not for himself, but for his country, and still more for his church. Without selfishness or loose passions, he was worthy to be a prelate of Imperial Rome, and a statesman of Imperial Spain. While clad in the almost regal robe of a cardinal, he still wore beneath it the mean coarse robe of his order, and this was a fit type of his life, for while the one prefigured his vast power, the other still more aptly signified the lifelong martyrdom of a soul that longed to be free—a martyrdom, Christians tell us, that showed itself in the lines of a noble face furrowed with care and sorrow." God bless such princes! Even though the preachers denounce them, they shine as the stars forever!

ASTRONOMY.

Cardinal Ximines only built upon ancient Catholic foundations, in the science of astronomy, when he gave the Gregorian calendar, which England and Russia rejected from religious prejudice, but have lately been compelled to accept. The Pope had always patronized and fostered this science. Virgilius demonstrated the rotundity of the earth in the midnight of what the preachers call "Roman superstition." For his piety and astronomical discoveries he was made bishop of Madgeburg by the very dignitary who, according to Jasper and other preachers, "was always agin science, and denied dat de sun do move."

Before Luther apostatized, Copernicus taught at Rome, and left a system of astronomy which Galileo assisted in developing. Even his genius was also fostered by the Pope, but when, like a goose, he began to hiss at the Bible and meddle with theology, the Inquisition imprisoned him for three days, and then shot him out with the admonition and warning: *Sutor, crepitat, sutorem.*—(See Jeff' Davis' idea, p. 40.)

Before the 16th century astronomy and maritime science had already made astonishing advances. Behold, O great America—even if other nations despise and spit upon Him—behold your true Saviour, your native home, and fly to the bosom of your holy mother, the Catholic Church! Prince Henry of Portugal, surnamed "The Navigator," had erected his observatory at Cape St. Vincent. Cardinal D'Ailey had written his *Imago Mundi*, which instructed a little boy named Christopher Columbus, at Palos, in Italy! Tosconnelli from the tower of St. Mary's Church, in Florence, had studied the heavens and written letters of encouragement to the great discoverer. Father Juan Perez now pleads the cause of science and Christianity before Isabella, and Christopher Columbus, under the patronage of a Catholic queen, kneels down upon the shores of San Salvador exclaiming:

"*O Lord God, Eternal and Omnipotent, who by thy Divine Word hast created the heavens, the earth, and the sea! Blessed and glorified be thy Name, and praised thy Majesty who hast deigned by me, Thy humble servant, to have that sacred Name made known and preached in this other part of the world!*"

Then, rising with majesty and displaying the standard of the Cross, he solemnly offered to God the first fruits of his discovery, named the island San Salvador, (Holy Saviour,) and gave orders for a large cross to be constructed.

O, thou grand and beautiful and free—fair-minded America! Look upon your father; behold your mother! They approach your great centennial—*eighteen hundred and eighty-two!* Kneel thou, in humble reverence, at their feet; and if miscreants dare to buffet them—but you know your duty; I know your HEART! See Anarchy on one side, and the Catholic church on the other. Only two great parties now remain. *Americus* Vespucius comes with Columbus to gaze upon your greatness. He lays his hand upon your flashing sword, O, brave America, and thus repeats your name—perhaps foretells your destiny: "America! America!! daughter of Heaven and child of Faith, behold your heritage! *Defend the Truth!* Though the kings of the earth may court the mob and reject the Vicar of Christ, behold, he crowns a young republic! Not only your hills and valleys shout for joy, but hosts of angels sing your triumph, and forty million martyrs call you blessed!"

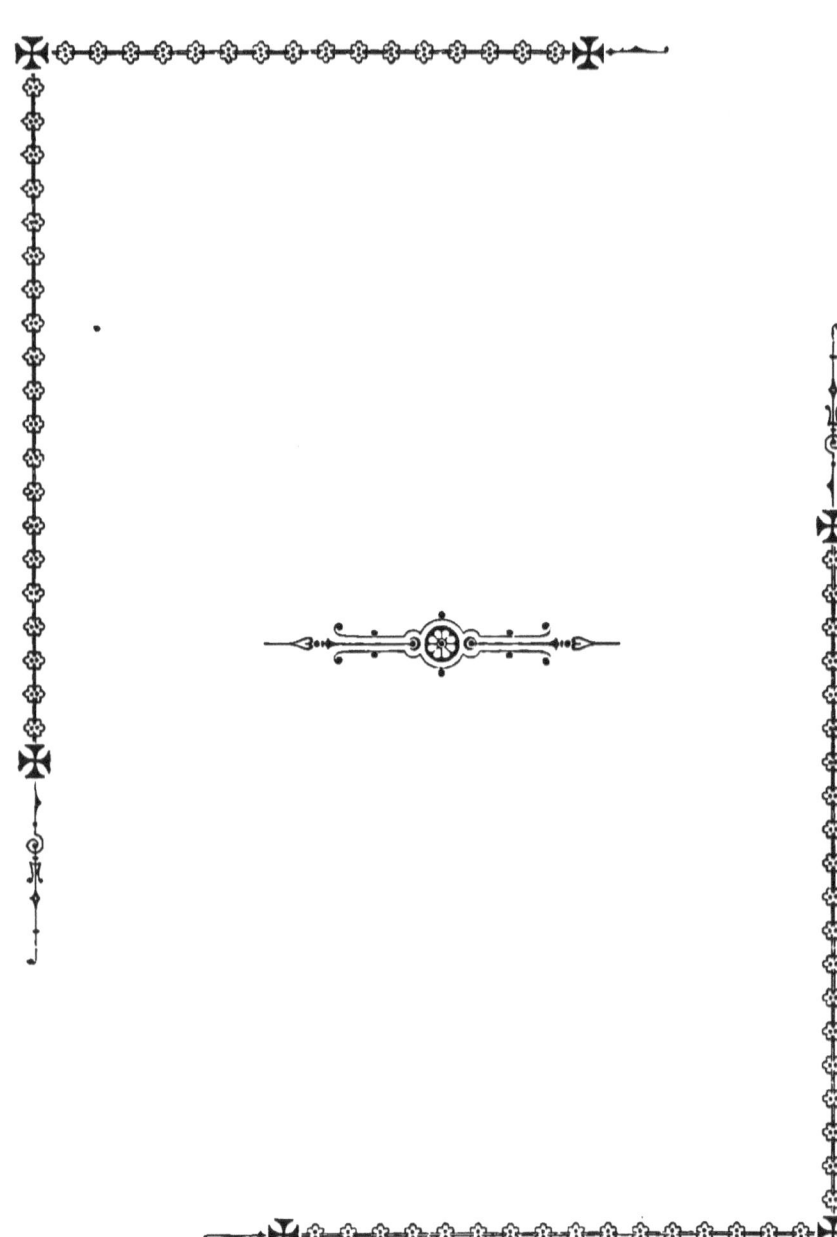

www.ingramcontent.com/pod-product-compliance
Lightning Source LLC
Chambersburg PA
CBHW021949160426
43195CB00011B/1289